I HEARD HER
CALL MY NAME

ALSO BY LUCY SANTE

Nineteen Reservoirs

Maybe the People Would Be the Times

The Other Paris

Folk Photography

Novels in Three Lines

Kill All Your Darlings

The Factory of Facts

Evidence

Low Life

I HEARD HER CALL MY NAME

A Memoir of Transition

Lucy Sante

PENGUIN PRESS ◯ NEW YORK ◯ 2024

PENGUIN PRESS
An imprint of Penguin Random House LLC
penguinrandomhouse.com

LIBRARY OF CONGRESS CATALOGING-IN-PUBLICATION DATA
Names: Sante, Lucy, author.
Title: I heard her call my name : a memoir of transition / Lucy Sante.
Description: New York : Penguin Press, 2024.
Identifiers: LCCN 2023019672 (print) | LCCN 2023019673 (ebook) |
ISBN 9780593493762 (hardcover) | ISBN 9780593493779 (ebook)
Subjects: LCSH: Sante, Lucy. | Transgender people—Biography.
Classification: LCC HQ77.8.S353 A3 2024 (print) | LCC HQ77.8.S353 (ebook) |
DDC 306.76/80092 [B]—dc23/eng/20230830
LC record available at https://lccn.loc.gov/2023019672
LC ebook record available at https://lccn.loc.gov/2023019673

Printed in the United States of America
1st Printing

Designed by Alexis Farabaugh

Beware of all enterprises that require new
clothes, and not rather a new wearer of clothes.

HENRY DAVID THOREAU, *WALDEN*

Between February 28 and March 1, 2021, I sent the following text as an email attachment to around thirty people I considered my closest, most consistent, day-to-day friends. While I sent the emails out individually, the subject line was usually the same: "A bombshell." I smirked at the unintentional pun and wondered whether anyone else would. It was simply titled "Lucy."

The dam burst on February 16, when I uploaded Face-App, for a laugh. I had tried the application a few years earlier, but something had gone wrong and it had returned a badly botched image. But I had a new phone, and I was curious. The gender-swapping feature was the whole point for me, and the first picture I passed through it was the one I had tried before, taken for that occasion. This time it gave me a full-face portrait of a Hudson Valley woman in midlife: strong, healthy, clean-living. She also had lovely flowing chestnut hair and a very subtle makeup job. And her face was mine. No question about it—nose, mouth, eyes, brow, chin, barring a hint of enhancement here or there. She was me. When I saw her I felt something liquefy in the core of my body. I trembled from my shoulders to my crotch. I guessed that I had at last met my reckoning.

Very soon I was feeding every portrait and snapshot and ID-card picture I possessed of myself into the magic gender portal. The first archival picture I tried, contemporaneous with my first memory of staring into a mirror and arranging my hair and expression to look like a girl, was an anxious, awkward studio portrait of a tween, all cowlicks and baby fat. The transformed result was a revelation: a happy little girl. Apart from her long black hair, very little had been done to transform Luc into Lucy; the biggest difference was how much more relaxed she looked. And so it generally went—I was having a much better time as a girl in that parallel life. I passed every era through the machine, experiencing one shock of recognition after another: That's *exactly* who I would have been. The app sometimes returned blandly misjudged or grotesquely distorted images, but more often than not it weirdly seemed to guess what my hairstyle and fashion choices would have been in those years. The less altered the resulting images were, the deeper they plunged a dagger into my heart. That could have been me! Fifty years were under water, and I'd never get them back. My high-school graduation portrait, a haughty near-profile, hair waving off the brow and into a curl, became an impossibly delicate almond-eyed fawn (age 17 was indeed the summit of my beauty, which is probably why my male incubus immediately grew a beard). Ten or twelve years later (there are regrettably few photos of me in my 20s; I've always been camera-shy), I am a Lower East Side postpunk radical lesbian anarcha-feminist with a Dutch-boy bob and a pout. Here I am at a *Sports Illustrated* junket in Arizona, age 33, looking demure in a white sweater over a red polka-dot dress, talking to a boy.

There are many reasons why I repressed my lifelong desire to be a woman. It was, first of all, impossible. My parents would have called a priest and had me committed to some monastery, *lettre de cachet*–style. And the culture was far from prepared, of course. I knew about Christine Jorgensen when I was fairly young, but she seemed to be an isolated case. Mostly what you came across were aggressively vile jokes from Vegas comedians and the occasional titillating tabloid story. Nobody felt threatened by transgender people; on the contrary, they were viewed as hilarious sideshow acts—literally and otherwise, as in Weegee's photographs. I kept searching for images or stories of girls like me, without much luck. I would swoon over pictures from Finocchio's or Club 82 I might find in passing, but their stars mostly seemed to be gay men who changed back into male drag after the show. Over the years I consumed an impressive amount of material on transgender matters, from clinical studies to personal accounts (where are you, circa-1984 issue of *Actuel*—or was it *The Face?*—that nearly broke my mind?), to new-journalistic exposés to porn. Not much of the porn, though; it grossed me out. I researched the subject as deeply as I did any of my books, but my notes all had to be kept in my head.

I immediately disposed of all materials, because I was terrified of being seen. When with some regret I threw away a pseudo-scientific piece of exploitation called *The Transvestites*, I made sure to bury it in the center of the trash bag. Until browsers made anonymous searching possible, I wiped the search memory on my computer every day. Why, you may ask, did I feel it necessary to go to such lengths? The short answer is that I'm mildly paranoid about writings on paper (or screen) because my mother regularly raided my room, reading anything in my handwriting and vetting all printed matter for anything that might even remotely allude to sex. I extended that caution to my friends, most of whom would surely have been sympathetic, because of the notion I long possessed that women would be disgusted and repelled by my transgender identity. Where did I get that one? It may be because until I was in my late teens I didn't know many women, as an only child of isolated immigrants, and although I had one early romantic interest, I didn't have a female friend until I was seventeen. It may also very well have come from proto-TERF sentiments I picked up from feminist tracts. Needless to say, I was awful at sex. I did not know how to act like a man in bed. I wanted to see myself as a woman in the act of love, but I also had to repress the desire, while simultaneously trying earnestly to please my partner (because I almost never slept with anyone I didn't love at least at first). Most of the time, the mass of contradictions prevented me from any but the most mechanical sexual fulfillment, and necessarily impeded my companion's pleasure as well.

I was not at all attracted to men, and I spent enough time in gay environs in the '70s to be sure of that. At puberty and afterward I was uncertain how to construct a masculine identity. I hated sports and dick jokes and beer-chugging and the way men talked about women; my idea of hell was an evening with a bunch of guys. Over the years, from force of necessity, I created a male persona that was saturnine, cerebral, a bit remote, a bit owlish, possibly "quirky," coming very close to asexual despite my best intentions. During those same years I thought about my trans identity every single day, sometimes all day long. I had a range of masturbation scenarios: cast as a girl in the school play, then persuaded to go out on the town in costume; hired as an assistant by a wealthy society woman who amuses herself by dressing me up as a girl; new roommate assigned to me in college has been dressing as a girl for years and has a full wardrobe. Yes, they were transvestite fantasies, but that was what seemed available. Just the idea of wearing women's clothes made me dizzy, and I can count the number of times I dressed up (furtively, alone) on the fingers of one hand. I looked lovely, but I felt as though the entire world was looking on in contempt or repulsion or dire judgment. But then I couldn't just wish myself into magically becoming a girl, could I? And when I truly probed my desire to have breasts and a vagina I was suffused with an existential terror.

Another reason for my repression was my sense that if I changed my gender it would obliterate every other thing I wanted to do in my life. I wanted to be a significant writer, and I did not want to be stuffed into a category, any category. At first, writing seemed to be a pursuit where one could hone a persona with words while evading inspection in the flesh, but marketing changed that, brutally, beginning in the '80s; I could no longer hide there, and if I were transgender that fact would be the only thing anyone knew about me. Over the years, transgender people became gradually more visible in the media, and the coverage became a little bit less snide. I lived in New York City, so I saw transgender people often: the doo-wop group that lived as women in

the Whitehall Hotel on 100th Street, the two very pol-
ished party girls in tiger prints I saw one early morning
in the subway. A few years later I passed through the
same circles as Greer Lankton and Teri Toye, although
I was too scared to ever talk to them; they seemed like
mythological creatures come to earth. For that matter
I was close for a while to Nan Goldin, who would
have been certain to understand my story, but I never
breathed a word. I would hear rumors that this or that
person "dressed up," and I would be forever ill at ease in
their presence as a result—from envy, of course. My office in the late eighties and early nineties was a block
from Tompkins Square Park, but I never so much as
peeked in at Wigstock (I could hear it), and half a block
from the Pyramid Club, but I never went there, either,
except maybe to see some band. In those days the club
had a black menu board on the sidewalk outside that
read "Drink and be Mary." I trembled every time I
passed it. I'd occasionally see skits on the UHF porn
channel by persons calling themselves "chicks with
dicks," and know they were somewhere in my neighborhood, maybe very close by. In the late nineties I was invited to the dinner after Nan's Whitney opening, and
seated at my table was the glorious Joey Gabriel; I'm not

sure I spoke a word during the whole course of the evening.

I was terrified, that is, of finding myself confronted by what I am confronting now. Somehow now the dam has burst, the scales have fallen away, the fog has lifted. The various lists above give but a small idea of the vast scope of my investment in my transgender identity. I absorbed every factoid, every anecdote, every historical specula-tion, every scabrous rumor pertaining to the matter of boys changing into girls. I continually conjured up, rev-eled in, and suppressed images of myself as a woman. It was the consuming furnace at the center of my life. And yet, until these past few weeks, my repression kept me from seeing the phenomenon as a coherent whole. I wanted with every particle of my being to be a woman, and that thought was pasted to my windshield, and yet I looked through it, having trained myself to do so. Now that the floodgates have opened I am consumed by the thought in a new way. I have spoken frankly to my thera-pist about it, making her the first human being (after nine or ten previous shrinks) to hear those things from my lips. That gives the matter the force of reality. When I up-loaded my first picture to FaceApp I felt liquid and melt-ing in the core of my body. Now I feel a column of fire.

That should not, however, imply a steely resolve. Now that I have opened Pandora's box, I cannot close it again, but have no idea what to do with the specters it has let loose. The idea of transitioning is endlessly seductive and endlessly terrifying. I take at least one selfie every day and transform it, and it feels as though the pictures are becoming ever more plausible. Yes, that's clearly my face, every bit of it—my features are fortunately disposed, and even the contours of my face are not excessively large. With a bit of makeup, a course of estrogen, and a really nice wig I could look exactly like that, maybe. But will the fact that I can't grow my own hair make me feel like a fake forever? It doesn't take much to make me feel fake—the much improved social climate of the present, the very thing that has made this recent epiphany at all possible, also makes me think that others will see me as merely following a trend, maybe to stay relevant. And I am soon to turn 67. What if I look like a grotesque? Or merely pathetic? While I know that my friends and the people I know in publishing and the arts would be sympathetic, and that my main employer is exceptionally trans-friendly, I worry about private reactions. I myself have not always been kind when someone in public life or on the periphery of my social orbit has transitioned in ways I thought less than successful or less than dignified. I'm worried about having the talk with my son, although like many members of his generation he has transgender friends and is very open to the subject. Most of all I worry about telling my partner, with whom I've shared an affectionate relationship that has slowly become more companionate over the past fourteen years. I don't doubt her sympathy, but can also imagine her asking what her role might be, as if to say that I am living out a love affair with myself. And would she feel comfortable with my wearing feminine clothes and accessories while she wears mostly T-shirts and jeans?

It's a vast decision, with the power to affect every aspect of my life. Would I inadvertently destroy important things in my life as a consequence? I think about transitioning incessantly, look at sites for wigs and makeup and clothing as if I were actually shopping and not simply stocking the larder of my imagination. If it weren't for COVID-19 I would contrive some way of paying a visit to a transformation salon, but those places are all closed now. I keep wanting to be forced to transition by some circumstance, maybe my therapist telling me that it is crucial for my sanity. Anyway I'm starting here, by

writing it down—something I've never done before—
and by sending it to a very few people whom I trust and
who I think will understand. My name is Lucy Marie
Sante, only one letter added to my deadname.

26 February 2021

That was written from within a whirlwind. I am astonished anew
every time I consider the chronology. The first FaceApp manifestation occurred February 16. Ten days later I came out to my
therapist, Dr. G., who didn't blink, but merely said she thought transitioning made sense and was a good idea. The following evening,
after I'd written the letter, I came out to my partner, Mimi, which
was the single most difficult thing of them all, and the day after that
I came out to my son, Raphael. The fortification of secrets I'd spent
nearly sixty years building and reinforcing had crumbled to dust in
a little over a week. The letter itself was so conclusive that it would
serve as the template for the formal public coming-out piece that
I'd write in October and see published in *Vanity Fair* the following
February. By feeding the snapshots of my life into the maw of the
photo-altering software, I managed to force open a door in my subconscious, one festooned with padlocks and wax seals and warning
signs in nineteen languages. That was not a reversible action. Opening it released a flood of matter—knowledge, speculation, dreams—

that had been confined so long it had fermented and become hallucinogenic. I never had to face the usual question confronting people who transition earlier in life: Am I really trans? That question had been decided for me decades earlier, as much as I fought against acknowledging it.

The reaction was immediate: emails, phone calls, texts. Everyone was nice, although there was a range. There was "unexpected but not surprising" and "surprised but not surprised" and "shocking but not" at one end, and at the other were a few people who reacted as if they'd been hit by a train while they were looking the other way. Those tended mainly to be guys who over the course of many years' friendship had come to think of me as a sort of mirror or alter ego, so reevaluating me meant having to reevaluate themselves. Everybody on the "not surprised" end was female, as were the three persons who wrote to say they had happy tears in their eyes as they read my letter. When sending the letter to one close friend of nearly fifty years, who is gay, I reminded him that he had once compared gender transition to "a kind of suicide." In his response he admitted he "took the condition as somehow a threat to gaydom, but that was when I knew nothing, and I mean nothing, about trans. Drag and cross-dressing were treated as extensions of gay, and they are not at all the same thing."

I felt as though I needed to send the letter to at least one trans person, and there was none in my circle, so I sent it to a trans woman on the West Coast I knew at one or two removes. Her life was too busy to allow her to finish reading the letter, but after a cursory examination of the first page she wrote: "My only note so far is that I wouldn't mention your crotch in connection with a realization about your gender identity, because any mention of genitalia or crotches instantly brings up all sorts of bizarre paranoid delusions that trans women are just transitioning as part of some kind of sexual fetish." But this was merely a private letter addressed to a small group, I thought of writing back, but didn't. I changed the word to that Victorian euphemism, "belly." Another West Coast friend, a psychologist specializing in trans children and adolescents, wrote, "I am aware of the complications of a cis person commenting on a trans person's appearance, and comments about beauty and what it means to be feminine are landmines, so I'm hoping this is okay to say . . ." I had no idea there were complications to merely telling a friend they look nice.

I was prepared for some kind of pushback, softly and judiciously expressed, of course, but it never really came, then or later. The closest thing I got was an unimpeachably sincere letter from a very serious friend: "I am . . . concerned about the suddenness of this insight. And while that doesn't invalidate its truth, as a friend, I would ask that before you make any irrevocable medical decisions you give this a bit of time to see how it feels." I wondered if he thought that one day I'd hop on the steamer to Casablanca and reappear six months later as the Louisiana Firecracker. But most responses were yay, go for it, you do you. The men often felt it necessary to congratulate me on my courage, as if that were even an operative term. As the months went by and I came out to concentric rings of friends and acquaintances my correspondence grew mightily. I heard from people who had heard indirectly: former students, onetime colleagues, long-ago editors, people who'd had me read in their series once, people from deep in my past who preserved a certain 1973 party in their memory as if it were a pear in eau-de-vie. New categories of response were added. My favorites were the "secret sharer" notes, from cis men who had felt a twinge, or more than a twinge, and had hidden it away for reasons similar to mine but were determined to keep on doing so, yet still felt a little wistful.

Sometime in the early weeks of my transition I began hearing snatches of a song in my head, a song I had written the words to. Or rather, a prose poem I wrote in 1978, when I was twenty-four, that a couple of years later was set to music by Phil Kline and eventually recorded by the Del-Byzanteens, a band that also included

Jim Jarmusch, Philippe Bordaz, and Jamie Nares, all friends of mine. The poem was called "Easy Touch," although for some reason I changed the title for the song version to "Girls Imagination." I had seen on the UK charts a listing for a lovers rock girl-group cover of the Temptations' "Just My Imagination," which was titled "Girls Imagination." The group was called 15-16-17, after their ages. I was charmed by the title's missing apostrophe, which made it interestingly ambiguous: it could represent the imagination of one or more girls, or refer to the way the imagination is set off by girls, or indeed equate the propositions "girls" and "imagination." My friends' song, a trancelike western raga after the manner of the Kinks' "See My Friends," appeared on a twelve-inch single and the one album by the Del-Byzanteens, and on the soundtrack of a film by Wim Wenders, *The State of Things.*

I rarely thought about it anymore. When songs drifted into my internal airspace for no good reason—I hadn't heard them at the

supermarket or the movies or on my iPod—I always wondered why they would choose that moment to climb into my head. In this case the words came back to me as if they had been written by someone else, and I turned them over as I mentally replayed them.

There was a remarkable slow movement she did with her hands, circling halves of what would have been her face, as if trying to mold one out of ectoplasm. The ruined girly look she wore was completely the effect of the thin cream plastic mask that sat over. Pulling away, a robe would leave imprints on newly grafted skin, so strange to be someone lifelike but too early. First movies became longer and longer, and then movies loved her back.

It was the beginning of a new dream which was real life, or the manifestation of an old one at its cusp. She imagined they took her in a white car to a room in a club and the touch was given to her. The other women looked back at her, but they were sisters under the mink. She threw off the red cape and sang:

> *There's no use walking in just a shirt*
> *When baby's got on her animal feet,*
> *And there's no point to a lot of business*
> *When what you mean is nobody home.*

Then they pulled on the cords attached to her legs and she became bigger and bigger. Then bluish fingernails on soft, sticky piano keys.

I was stunned. The whole thing was about transitioning! How had that passed my internal censor? At the time I thought I was weaving a vague reverie based on two movies, *Eyes Without a Face* by Georges Franju and *The Big Heat* by Fritz Lang; the "thin cream plastic mask" comes from the first and "sisters under the mink" from the second. Both films feature the disfigurement of the female protagonist. I've always been frankly in awe of my subconscious, which pulls off the damnedest things when least expected. If I were in a 12-step program it would be my higher power. Here it had smuggled in a whole scenario I had rarely managed to explore even in the privacy of my own imagination, as terrified as I was of the implications. I shivered at the words "so strange to be someone life-like but too early," which perfectly described the state I found myself in then, and sometimes still do. It was nothing less than a founding myth, a sort of robing of the bride, an alchemical transformation from male to female, sealed by the recognition and approval of other women. And is that actually a clitoris in the last sentence?

My subconscious was attuned to my being and my desires in a way that my conscious mind couldn't afford. The sophistication of my repressive mechanism can be gauged by the fact that I was able to write those words, show them to my friends, hear them set to music, hear them sung live dozens of times and on record in two formats, print them in a chapbook I made of my early poetry in 2009—and not once tumble to their real subject, which seems unmistakable to me now. For that matter, look at the refrain of the other song I wrote for the Del-Byzanteens, the title track of their album *Lies to Live By*: "If I only have one life, let me live it as a lie." Note that it hijacks a ubiquitous Clairol commercial from the 1970s: "If I only have one life, let me live it as a blonde." The conflict is spelled out so explicitly you'd think I would have noticed.

Who am I? is a question I've been trying to resolve for the better part of my life, even without reference to matters of gender. The putative answer is both specific and elusive. I'm a writer before I'm anything else. I'm European and American, poised midway between those poles in both attitude and citizenship status. I'm a Walloon, pretty much 100 percent, a thoroughbred specimen of one of the world's more overlooked ethnic groups, overlooked in part because they seldom seem to stray from home. (Over the course of fifty years I've met no more than three in the United States.) I'm an only child, with few surviving relatives. I'm a father of one. I'm an ex-boyfriend and an ex-husband twice. I'm a retired professor (very part-time at that). I'm a visual artist in seasons when the visual-arts moon is high in the sky. I'm a homeowner. I'm a registered Democrat, but my political leanings range somewhat left of that—although everything is such a mess now that I no longer bother trying to specify exactly where. I'm not a member of any club or organization, except a hundred-member online chat group I joined at its start in 2007.

I'm down to about five feet, ten inches; I'm into the shrinking years. I try to keep my weight as near to 150 pounds as I can manage. I don't know my blood type, which is shocking at my age. I've had surgical interventions on my spine (sciatica) and my left knee, but everything in my body seems in working order, knock on wood. My only recurrent problem is kidney stones, which I've had since I was fifteen and which lie in wait to surprise me at inopportune moments, such as publication day of a big book, with the promo tour starting the next day. I have patrician toes, can roll my tongue and cock one eyebrow; can't whistle for shit, though. I am bald. I'm partially colorblind. I'm afraid of heights. I love to walk and swim, but have never voluntarily pursued sports. I smoked cigarettes (mostly roll-ups, mostly Gauloises tobacco) for thirty years, and quit because of a small persistent cough that my doctor laughingly assured me was hay fever, when I finally consulted her after two years of it. I nevertheless continue to consume nicotine on a daily basis, initially via gum (yuck) and then e-cigarettes that look enough like filter tips that waitresses on Parisian terraces come running with lighters. I've also consumed cannabis daily for more than fifty years. I barely drink. I alternate periods of decent sleep and periods of insomnia, which I medicate. I eat pretty much everything, although there was no refrigerator or fast food in my first six years, so I don't go for convenience. I do my own cooking.

I'm old-school in a great many ways. I identify as a bohemian, and I should maybe have put that at the top if it weren't that there are vanishingly few actual bohemians walking around today, and by now I am bourgeois despite my best efforts. I never forget that I come from the working class; class has interfered with more than one of my intimate relationships. I have no religious or spiritual beliefs, perhaps because I was brought up in strict and even fanatical Catholic observance. I'm a romantic. I'm basically a scofflaw, and have no patience with literal-mindedness. I have no academic degrees. I'm profoundly nostalgic for the analog era, but even more my nostalgia is for the time before Ronald Reagan and Margaret Thatcher ushered in the present sociopathic moral culture, devoted to the destruction of community and the devaluation of human beings, which grew all-pervasive with the coming of the digital era. I'm urban, concrete, disabused. I rely on humor to keep me sane. I love all kinds of music, but sometimes I like silence even more. (I am, after all, a writer.)

I was born on May 25, 1954, in Verviers, Belgium, the only child of Lucien Mathieu Amélie Sante and Denise Lambertine Alberte Marie Ghislaine Nandrin. My father was the only son of older parents, an heir to a local tradition of working-class self-education, a laborer who had stepped up to a managerial role at an iron foundry,

a worker who felt pulled in various aspirational directions—the theater above all—but had determined to settle down and provide for a
family, a matter about which he nursed reservations he kept locked
in a triple-walled emotional safe. My mother was the only daughter
of tenant farmers who lost their lease at the start of the worldwide
Depression and were forced to move to the city and take factory jobs.
She was anchored by her piety, which was overwhelming and at the
same time very simple, against a sea of torments.

I was born an only child. That is, my mother was warned, after
my safe birth, not to try it again. She had suffered several miscarriages and, a year and a month before me, a stillbirth. My parents
each had one sibling—of the opposite sex, symmetrically—neither
of whom had children, so I had no first cousins. I had no cousins at
all on my father's side, because my grandfather was the youngest
and came to procreation much later than his brothers, so that my
father's first cousins were thirty years older; they didn't mingle. My
mother's cousins, who constituted most of her social life, had stayed
in the country, and out there they produced children at calendar
intervals. I had so many first cousins once removed I couldn't keep
them straight or manage to get close to any. My concept of family
was, besides my parents, primarily a matter of the older generation:
my three surviving grandparents—all of them dead before I turned
nine—and my robust, good-humored, briskly intelligent, deeply
kind, pie-baking Tante Fonsine, who lived long enough that I visited

her on my Eurail Pass when I was twenty, surely the only time I ever voluntarily instigated a family visit.

Because of my mother's parents and their vast families, my early childhood featured holiday meals and group outings and Sunday afternoon coffee-and-cakes that were populated by a large and shifting cast of characters, some of whom I only sighted once or twice. I vividly remember meeting my cousin Myriam, Tante Fonsine's granddaughter, born in Kinshasa when it was still called Léopoldville, apparently the first pretty girl I had ever seen. We played together with my vast family of stuffed animals. Her eyes flashed and her smile filled the room. I may only have met her that one time, although I regularly sneaked looks at her photograph for years. But all the family hubbub, the exciting whirl of holiday activity, the time spent with my adoring grandmother, the door-to-door visits because nobody had a telephone—all of that went away in February 1959, when I was four and a half.

European industry was then near the beginning of a crisis that would span the following two or three decades. First coal was in trouble, then steel, then glass, paper, chemicals; the range of industries affected included the wool trade that had dominated my hometown since the start of the industrial revolution. When my father's place of employment was shuttered he faced the same dilemma as most other adult males of his time and place, most of whom saw just two options: to go on the dole, possibly for many years, or to relocate to the Congo, which for most of a century had been—scruples aside—a place where working-class Belgians could become management and live in villas, with servants. That did not appeal to my father at all, whether or not he could sense the imminent end of colonial rule, which finally occurred in 1961, and he had too much pride to collect unemployment.

But his childhood friend Lucy Dosquet had married an American GI after the war and moved with him to his native New Jersey. And then in 1953 her brother Pol, my dad's best friend, had followed with his wife; they were among the very last immigrants to be processed at Ellis Island. Pol got a job at the Summit, New Jersey, plant of the Swiss pharmaceutical firm Ciba, a really good job, he boasted, and claimed he could get my father one just as good. So, after many long columns of figures in my dad's tiny script on the backs of envelopes, my parents packed up their possessions and moved my mother's parents into our house. We set off in style: by airplane, quite expensive in those days, eleven and a half hours from Brussels to New York with a refueling stop in Montreal.

But the promise turned out to be a chimera. Pol's job was not the executive position he had claimed, but consisted of feeding and cleaning up after the experimental lab animals (for Easter that year I received a flock of baby chicks, which were then whisked away again), and he couldn't get a place for my dad. The only work my father could find was mowing lawns at another nearby plant for

$1.37 an hour. The Dosquets and my parents fought—the feud was to endure for forty years, while the two couples lived in adjacent towns and silently observed one another at the supermarket—and we moved out of their apartment. Every night my father sweated over his calculations.

So in October we headed back to Belgium. We took a Belgian freighter bound for Rotterdam—the rock-bottom cheapest way to travel in those days—and after stowing our baggage decided to tour New York City, since we hadn't seen it yet and might not have another chance. It was Halloween, a holiday then unknown to Europeans. In New York City in 1959, it meant wild hordes of children in bedsheets and witches' hats running unchaperoned through the streets. I was agog; I had seen utopia. I had also seen the lurid signage that spilled forth from the Forty-second Street movie houses in those pre-porn days, despite my mother—who saw smut everywhere she looked—keeping my chin in her hand and pointing it out toward the curb. Times Square sleaze, too, then became an emblem of freedom for me, even if I had no idea what it was about. Thus was born the legend of New York City in my mind. Long before I would have been able to articulate any of it, the city awakened in me the very earliest notions I had of autonomy and independence and adventure. For the first time, the jail door was briefly left ajar.

Back in Belgium my father managed to land a decent job, but evidently the tensions between him and my mother's parents, now

our tenants, became too hard to bear—I have no memories at all from those ten months. By August we were back in the States, by October back in Summit. The pattern of yo-yoing never quite ceased. Although my father, who had few living ties, was perfectly content to stay in the US, my mother never lost the desperate wish to go back to Belgium. In 1962 she and I went back because my grandmother was dying, and the following year because my grandfather was in dire straits. Both visits ran for months—my second and third grades were split between American and Belgian schools—as my mother tried and failed to make a case for moving back permanently. I ended up feeling as if I had immigrated to the United States four times. Finally in 1988, after my father retired, they pulled up stakes and caused a prefab house to be erected on land next to my mother's cousin Nelly, in the rural village of Saint-Hubert, where my father had nothing to look at and nothing to do. Two years later they were back in New Jersey, in a house a block away from where they'd lived before, where my father chiefly looked at football and golf on TV.

When my father retired, my parents had asked for my advice in choosing among three options: stay in New Jersey, go back to Belgium, or move to Florida. I advised Belgium, since I had spent more than twenty-five years listening to my mother's pining. Even so my mother, as she later told me, suspected that part of my motive was to be rid of them—she wasn't wrong—so she punished me by throwing away all my belongings that remained in their house, and those were most of the tangible remnants of my childhood and adolescence. That typified the dynamic between my mother and me: the passive aggression, the bottled-up rage, the ability to get under each other's skin. It hadn't always been that way, of course. I was the miracle child, and appropriately cherished.

$\circ$

Less than two weeks after sending out the "Lucy" letter, I wrote a second letter to the same crowd.

> It's been a hell of a month. Well, it's been just shy of a month since the full load of gender dysphoria, which I'd secured in the deepest subcellars of my psyche since childhood, suddenly burst full-force upon me. It was profound, earthshaking, vivid. You may not think of me as impulsive, in part because I seldom show much of myself to others, but I am that, and so I immediately went all the way. Coming out to all of you was my crossing of the Rubicon. Airing my secret was liberating, and also irreversible. I thrilled at the prospect of dangling myself over what might be an abyss.
>
> And then I went farther. I bought wigs (four in total), breast forms, lingerie, clothing, and makeup. I lost nearly

ten pounds. I shaved off all my body hair. I moisturized religiously. I practiced female body language. I took voice lessons online. I joined at least six transgender forums or chat rooms, and earnestly contributed. Nearly every day the mail would bring another shipment of clothes—mostly cheap polyester things because I was navigating between my tastes and what would actually look good on me at my great age, and I didn't know what would take and what wouldn't. This all peaked when, wearing my deliciously thick and wavy Brazilian human-hair wig and my ankle-length long-sleeved black velvet dress, I made an appointment with an endocrinologist.

But I won't keep that appointment. I had been stifling my doubts, insisting to myself that I'd never been as certain of anything as of my desire to become a woman. But that very insistence was a clue to the fragility of my impulse. I went to bed last night with the doubts getting louder and more difficult to ignore, and when I woke up this morning the fever had broken. It's over. Maybe not for all time but for now. I've packed away all my gear and stowed it, perhaps appropriately, in the closet.

It was too much, too fast, and far too absolute. I wasn't ready, and I may never be. The process violated my innate sense of the dialectic, or perhaps I just mean my fundamentally dual personality—not that I believe in astrology, but I am after all a Gemini. Most importantly, I could not ignore the effect this was having on Mimi, whom I love more than I've ever loved anyone. She was a good sport and a real help, but my project had shifted things between us, and not only did I fear losing her, I found that I couldn't square Lucy's drive for euphoria with the deep bond between us, which has survived any number of crises over the past fourteen years.

And so, what now? I'm too old and too bald to be gender-fluid; also given my age I'm instinctively—perhaps wrongly—dualistic. I have little doubt that my impulse will reawaken, perhaps at intervals. I'm not throwing anything away. I may cross-dress now and then, maybe even around other people. Lucy lives on inside me and always will. Maybe someday I'll even keep an appointment with an endocrinologist. I really don't know what my psyche has in store for me. But that's the way I've always been. For example, I couldn't write—anything—if I knew in advance what was actually going to happen on the page. I move through life guided mainly by chance and a belief in negative capability. It's not the steadiest or most bankable procedure, but I can't help that.

The first manifestation of deep doubt this past month came when I started making a list of the great women— whom I've known or idolized from afar or after death— whose company I was excited to join. *I do not deserve to be in that number,* I thought, every time I added a name to the list. After all, I have benefited from male privilege for almost 67 years. I have never been overlooked or shunted aside because of my gender. My authority is male, as is my voice, literally and on the page. And although I'm well aware that gender and sex are two different things, I can't help but think that I've never faced breast or uterine cancer or vaginal infections or for that matter menopause. I'm certainly not making an argument against transgender transitioning. I've read and heard literally hundreds of often deeply moving personal accounts by people who found their real selves by evolving from one gender to another. But I'm not certain I qualify. I'm too thorny and various and contradictory and weird, and also, I can't help but think: I don't deserve it.

So I'm sticking with Luc for now. It's far from a perfect solution, but it's livable, perhaps especially in the light of my having come out to you all and the many things I've learned in the course of this feverish month. I may not be gender-fluid in the youth sense, but I feel emotionally expanded. One of the things I was most looking forward to from my anticipated course of anti-androgens and estrogen supplements was how my mind and heart would shift. I wanted the emotional range of a woman. I may never experience that, but maybe I can find some semblance of it within my deepest self. I will be in daily conversation with Lucy.

12 March 2021

The note was hooey, or largely so; it was a product of fear and grief. No doubt I was perfectly sincere about everything I wrote when I wrote it, but its semi-intentional task was to assist in a desperate flailing attempt to hold on to my fourteen-year relationship.

In a larger sense, it was caused by my inability to square my gender identity with my attraction to women. That had been the biggest problem all along. It contained an element of what I would learn is called "internalized transphobia." I had tried so hard for so long to be a heterosexual man that the need to behave like one took me over like a puppeteer whenever I found myself in the presence of a woman I found attractive. And that included a wide range of women on whom I had no sexual designs, from close friends to passing professional acquaintances. I needed to be a guy with them, so my body would automatically adjust: my jaw would drop, lengthening my face; my eyes would hood over; my shoulders would widen; I would regulate my walk. I knew how to do those things because I had studied movies.

But I had a hard time with the rest of the character. I modeled myself on my friends as best I could, but I wasn't privy to their pillow talk. It is only now that I can appreciate just how bad I was at being male, since I needed to kid myself to keep going. I craved physical intimacy, but the strictures of my upbringing prevented me from having much idea how to obtain it or what to do when I got there. I was not driven by my dick. It was ready and waiting, but didn't appear to know just what its role would be, clouded as that was by issues of gender and romance and equality. Sex was all yearning and mystery. There were times and circumstances when I fell in love every three minutes. Mostly I failed to score—to connect, I should say—with any of my intended, often because I gave up without even trying, so certain was I of rejection.

And yet paradoxically I felt attuned to women, relaxed in their presence, unburdened by the need to act male past a certain point. One reason my cousin Myriam loomed so large in my imagination for so long was because I hardly met any girls my age before my middle teens. When I finally did it was a revelation. With women I could talk and move and experience emotions without feeling like I needed to hold down an artillery position. By contrast, I experienced all men as competitors in a struggle I hadn't signed up for, the goal of which I couldn't fathom. Almost anything could count as a misstep; the rules were byzantine and changed constantly. Infractions were always punished, physically in childhood, by humiliation later on. There was always a hierarchical competition, from which I wanted to absent myself entirely. With women I could feel miles away from the war. They certainly had their own antagonistic social structures, but I didn't immediately see those. The women I started being friends with in my late teens were welcoming, generous, funny, with a calm appreciation of absurdity and a healthy disregard for the prevailing mindset. I could imagine myself as one of them—but the fantasy would shatter as soon as I realized that this could never happen.

I would fall short of women's expectations just as I had of men's, but this time it mattered more. The reaction would not be punishment but disappointment, which was worse. I would always be an awkward pretender, and as I learned about feminism more infractions were added: I was born without a cervix, would never menstruate, could never bear children. Women's childbearing capacity constituted a large percentage of their mercantile value, and hence was a primary target of their oppression. I could not suffer the way women suffer, so I could not qualify. And furthermore I was attracted to women, romantically and sexually, and that—in the sociocultural context of those years—made me a man whether or not I saw myself as one.

By the time I sent out my first letter the broader context had changed substantially. More people were aware that sex and gender do not necessarily correspond—that gender is in reality a very wide spectrum. Even before getting their reactions I had little doubt that the intelligent and independent women I knew would accept me. But I still desired women romantically, and I could not picture my feelings being reciprocated by anyone. I felt as if I were permanently exiling myself beyond love. The more I realized my thoroughgoing failure to play a male role in life—I had never really been a man at all—the more I sometimes wished my transition were going in the opposite direction. If I could become a man, maybe I could save my relationship. I would fit more easily into the world I lived in, which for better or worse was mostly made up of heterosexual couples. I could go on being who I'd pretended to be for sixty-six years, only now with all conflicts and contradictions painlessly resolved. The only problem was that I had opened Pandora's box. I didn't want to be a man.

But I didn't send that letter.

For three months I was on fire. I looked out at a world gone tilt. I was undergoing violent revolution. Every particle of my being was open to question, was minutely reviewed, was loudly debated, was denounced or redeemed. I was in a wind tunnel, blasted relentlessly by emotions, reflections, memories, sudden insights, minor epiphanies, things I didn't think I knew, angles I'd never considered. My body was a quivering mass of flying insects, each one fluttering to its own rhythm, setting off ripples that spread across my shoulders, down my spine from the brain stem, zigzagging through my arms and legs. I was turned inside out, flayed and reskinned, dissolved and rebuilt. I was face-to-face with the cosmos. The words *awe* and *dread*, previously abstractions, were suddenly alive in me. I spent days literally quaking. I felt like Bernini's Saint Teresa. "This cracks open the world," I wrote on an index card.

I've never kept a diary or journal, but during this whirlwind I started taking notes, just by way of touching ground every now and then. I went in for proclamations: "I have finally found my soul." "I'm already past the point of no return." "As a writer, I could imagine but I hadn't really lived. This is what was missing." "I'm so *relieved* I'm doing this." And then there was the inevitable counterpoint: "Do I deserve this?" Because I had been brought up to regard all instances of good fortune as unmerited, but also because I was proposing to join the ranks of women, and I didn't know that I could justify the presumption. I worried about integrating the many strands of my personality under this new heading. I immediately started worrying about my name, which was, in a sense, my shop sign. Would I be risking my public identity as a writer by changing it? (This seems trivial now, but the worry consumed me for months.)

I started compiling lists: exercises, clothing and shoe sizes, clubs and organizations, premonitory clues scattered willy-nilly across the landscape of my life. I searched back across the decades and noted down every cultural item with transgender implications that had crossed my path. John O'Hara's "The General," Faulkner's "Golden Land," Boris Vian's *Elles se rendent pas compte*, a few episodes in Jim Carroll's *Basketball Diaries*, a subplot in *Pimp* by Iceberg Slim. *Orlando*, by Virginia Woolf. Philippe d'Orléans and the Chevalier d'Éon; Bambi and Coccinelle. André Breton allegedly saying: "I wish that I could change my sex the way I change my shirt" (rather hard to believe in view of his sexual behavior and beliefs). The appearance of a movie called *I Want What I Want . . . to Be a Woman* at the Trans-Lux 86th Street maybe a week after I'd seen *2001: A Space Odyssey* there; I believe the tag line was "A plain boy becomes a beautiful woman." (No, I did not see the picture. Yes, I know the dates don't quite work, but that's how I remember it; I may be conflating two movies. I noticed the theater's name, familiar forever, as I was just now typing it out.)

My spotting a book called *Miss High-Heels* at the Marlboro Books franchise across the street from that theater. John Rechy's *City of Night*; Hubert Selby Jr.'s *Last Exit to Brooklyn*. Ads in *The Village Voice* for Michael Salem Boutique and Lee's Mardi Gras and the Gilded Grape; accounts in that paper of the Street Transvestite Action Revolutionaries (STAR)—like science fiction to me at the time. An account in the *Newark Evening News* of a runaway husband who turned up in the ticket booth of a porn theater in Florida, wearing a pink shift and ribbons in her hair. The nowadays unreadable Algonquin wit Alexander Woollcott, who in his youth "loved to dress up and pass himself off as a girl," and signed his letters "Alecia." Yearbooks from the 1920s and '30s at my all-boys high school, when the female parts in theatrical productions were all played by boys in drag. Was it possible that the model on the sleeve of Roxy Music's *For Your Pleasure* was a transsexual? (Yes, Amanda Lear.) When is a boy not a boy? (When he turns into a store.)

I was the baby who lived. I don't know much about my mother's gynecological woes, really. Such things were not discussed in my presence. But as soon as I was old enough to understand the adult world a bit—around age eight, maybe—I became fascinated with my parents' secrets. I knew they had them, but I could not figure out what they were, so I combed through their spoken words and their dresser drawers. Parsing their table talk, at some point I caught passing reference to what seemed like multiple instances of what I later learned were miscarriages. My parents married in February 1950. They were twenty-eight and twenty-six, late in life for their demographic, but that was the effect of the war and its impoverished aftermath. They would have started trying to procreate immediately, but the first time my mother carried to full term would not be until three years later. The certificate reads: "The year nineteen hundred fifty-three, the twenty-fifth of April, a lifeless child of the female sex was presented to us, taken from the womb of her mother." Her name, not indicated on the form, was Marie-Luce. My parents leased a cemetery plot, with no headstone, for ten years. When I was not quite nine her bones were removed to the ossuary.

The death certificate is the only proof I have that she existed at all, but she was nonetheless a living presence throughout my childhood. My mother could not let go of her. It may have been then that she began taking nerve pills that came in a metal tube; she was on assorted mood drugs for the rest of her life. There were frequent references in her talk to *la petite*, sometimes wistfully and sometimes maybe as if she were in the next room. At other times she seemed to think that I was her. She often called me by feminine diminutives: *ma fifille*, *ma chérie*, *ma choute* (because *chou* is masculine she had to confect a feminine form). Blue was for girls there and then, largely because of the Virgin Mary, but she dressed me in blue anyway, ostensibly because of her devotion to the Virgin. I too felt the presence of Marie-Luce, whose names I'd inherited in inverted order one year and one month later, but the form that presence took shifted around. Sometimes she was a phantom, sometimes she was my imaginary playmate and bedfellow, and sometimes she was me.

My parents' fortunes went up and down, up and down. They

were riding high when I was born, but then came a layoff or maybe a plant closure and they resigned themselves to running a Bata shoe franchise in a steel-mill town. When we'd come home from walks in the stroller my blanket would be speckled with soot. A year later things were on again, and that's when they bought a brand-new semidetached on a corner lot. It was a new development in a village where some of my mother's people had been living forever, now reinventing itself as a postwar suburb. For a year we even had a car, the first in the neighborhood, a Morris Minor. But modern amenities were few. We lacked central heating, hot running water, a refrigerator, a telephone—and so did everyone else. The walk down to the mezzanine toilet on a winter night was an arctic adventure, so the bedrooms were supplied with chamber pots. On visits after we'd moved to the US, when I was seven or eight, I'd come home from school for lunch and my mother would hand me a satchel, a list, and some money, and send me out to fetch the makings.

I was cosseted. I always had the best of everything, even when the family purse was slender. If my parents couldn't afford something, my maternal grandmother would figure out a way. She gave me a couple dozen Steiff animals, knitted me sweaters and scarves, knitted scarves for my Steiff animals. I have some notebooks my grandmother kept in her youth. Two of them, from her teens, are theological summations, and they are rigorous in their organization and penmanship, with cascades of indented curved brackets, like

legal writ. Another, from during the first war (as it was always called), when she was in her early twenties, is a collection of popular song lyrics, many of them alluding to England; maybe this was her way of resisting the Germans. She shocked her family by naming her children Denise and René—Parisian movie-star names at the time—and she changed her own name, from the antiquated Honorine to the more modern Anne-Marie. Clearly she could envision a world beyond the hardscrabble Ardennes farmland she came from. She was impatient with my mother, perhaps even cruel, giving her a lifelong inferiority complex, but she doted on me. I imagine I take after her.

Her husband scared me. After his wife's death he would sit and smoke his pipe, not turning on lights when it got dark, never reading or listening to the radio. Sometimes his brothers would come over and they would all sit in the dark, not talking. They were old farmers, with a concept of the world that did not range far beyond where they sat, although on our trips back they regularly called upon me to speak English for the benefit of the room (I can't imagine what kind of gibberish I might have emitted). They all terrified me, especially Achille, whose hawk nose was bent a quarter to the left. They represented something like an alien consciousness, utterly unfathomable to me. My mother told me flatly that her father was a coward. In May 1940, when they were fleeing Verviers on foot in advance of the Germans, intermittently being strafed by Stukas, my grandfather would always dive into the ditch without first assuring the safety of his wife and children. On the other hand I have a cabinet-card photo of him, circa 1912, from when he was briefly a streetcar conductor in Liège; he wears his uniform as if he were a major general.

Once in the USA for good, or semi-good, I seldom gave my Belgian relatives a thought. *Loin des yeux, loin du coeur*, the expression goes: far from the eyes, far from the heart. But then I was trying to bridge two cultures and two languages twice a day. At first there would be a buffer zone of about an hour between languages, when I wouldn't be able to speak either of them. For a year or two my mother gave me after-school French lessons so that I wouldn't lose my grasp, for which I am forever grateful. (She was a bigot. Everything Belgian—everything Walloon, more to the point—was the world's greatest, and the United States was a flashy, immoral, backward culture.) I began first grade without knowing a word of English; didn't know how to ask to go to the bathroom and so on. But I was squarely in the magic language window, and picked it up fast. The instruction was vivid—almost every word of basic English is even now accompanied in my mind by its history: the sign, label, decal, wrapper, billboard, truck body, junk mail, book, or newspaper where I first encountered it. I well remember my final triumph, when I leaped over the last hurdle: the day in fifth grade when I finally managed to pronounce "th," as in "three."

I was pretty much the only immigrant kid around. I remember a Hungarian family, refugees from the 1956 uprising, whose son

Laszlo was as palpably foreign as I was—we both earned school-yard jingles concerning this fact—but they didn't stick around. Most of a decade elapsed before I met another immigrant kid, a Cuban. The early 1960s was, in point of fact, the historical low for immigration to the United States; the postwar traffic from Europe had slowed and racist restrictions still barred much of the rest of the world. Which is to say that I was a curiosity, to be cautiously poked at. My practical education proceeded in fits and starts. I was always filled with questions I couldn't ask anyone: What does that slang word mean? Why is everybody wearing those things all of a sudden? What does anybody do after school? What is the goal of that game you're playing? Why did everybody laugh when that boy said that unfunny sentence? If I'd ever asked my schoolmates I would have been mocked and scorned. Maybe that happened once or twice, or maybe I was just anticipating.

I certainly couldn't ask my parents. They knew less than I did. My mother started to learn some English and a bit of the local mores a few years later when she went back to work, as a lunch lady at the local high school, but she remained baffled by much of American life and culture until the end. My father was less timid and much more of a cosmopolite, but he had found the job he would hold, with a few promotions along the way, for the last twenty-seven years of his working life—at a plant that made fluorocarbon coatings known in the trade as Teflon—and throughout my childhood and adolescence that entailed rotating shifts. We didn't always coincide when he worked evenings or nights. I didn't trust grown-ups at all, whether teachers or librarians or shopkeepers or kindly retired neighbors who gave me homemade magnets and obsolete encyclopedias. I had a handful of playmates in the neighborhood, a few schoolmates who were nice to me, but none of those friendships ran very deep. Fundamentally I was alone.

I guess that abiding aloneness is what allowed me to connect so strongly to the very first trans novel I read during my transition: *I Want What I Want*, by Geoff Brown. It was published in 1966 and may have been the first self-consciously literary effort to render the transgender experience. It was a late entry among the British "kitchen-sink" realist novels of the time, with authors like Nell Dunn, John Braine, Alan Sillitoe. Its author was a nice man who lived his whole life in the house he was born in, was married to the same woman for decades, wrote two novels (the other is from the perspective of a schizophrenic), and then gave up writing altogether. Whatever his inner life may have been like—his widow's comment was that he wanted to be anybody but Geoff Brown—he certainly got all the way inside the experience of transsexuality, rendering shades and nuances he could not easily have researched, at least not at the time.

The book tells the story of Roy, who has known all her life she is Wendy. But she lives in Hull, Yorkshire, with her father and stepmother, who run a fish-and-chips shop, and no one including her has any notion of transgender anything. She just knows she is not a homosexual or a cross-dresser; she is a woman. She steals some clothes and gets caught. Her father beats her, and she is sent to the mental hospital but checks herself out. Back at home, life remains troubled, with further clothes-stealing incidents and a continuing cycle of affection alternating with brutality. Finally, when she turns twenty-one and comes into a small bequest from her dead mother, she moves to a boardinghouse, and then another in a different neighborhood, transforming herself into Wendy, buying clothes by mail. She gradually builds a life for herself, and her gender change seems to be allowing her to transit social classes as well. I'll spoil the plot for you: she kills herself at the end. The reader could have seen this coming, perhaps before opening the book.

But that might be described as a history tax. The author is as beholden to the conventions of the age as his heroine. The tragic hermaphrodite really should have been a stock nineteenth-century melodrama character, and almost seems as if it had been. Anyway, the inner Hays Code so many of us carry around semiconsciously would naturally sentence such a creature to death, the price of deviance in most places and times. Wendy has had minimal schooling and knows only what she feels. She seems almost preindustrial, barely affected by movie imagery or any other kind of obvious template for her imagination. Everything she desires is based on women she has seen on the street, or sometimes has made up herself.

> A young girl walked on the footpath. Her hair was black. The breeze folded her summer dress as she walked. She walked along pretending to be unconscious of her happiness. There was something intelligent in her movements. Perhaps she was down on the long vacation from Oxford. Perhaps she was a clever model, come home for a rest from London. The first was possible. The second seemed unlikely. She was not tall enough. I was tall enough.

She is undereducated, but her inner monologues are often lyrical arguments of great complexity. Not very far into its pages I began copying out entire paragraphs in my notebook. I was struck by this passage, for example:

If I could get onto the other side, I would live happily with inhibitions in me because they would be the inhibitions of a woman. I wanted to be one of them. I did not want to stand apart and see them as fools. I wanted to be foolish with them. I wanted to suffer everything that they suffered. I wanted to be limited and mistaken. I wanted to be part of the world that was wrong instead of being shut in with my meaningless mathematics of thoughts that were right. A woman's body was a better place to live in than a man's brain. All real stuff was woman stuff. Mother and daughter and mother and daughter were one flesh going back in time to the female stomach creatures that needed no male. The male was outside. He might master the world, but he was not part of the world.

Wendy is unsophisticated but a complicated creature, with great depths of feeling in addition to an array of blind spots. The preceding passage traces a delicate tension of perspectives: Wendy's will, her irony, the author's irony. It must have been to some degree because the account is so exactingly specific about its heroine's inner life, not to mention her time and place, that it spoke to me so directly. For all our obvious differences, I could get into Wendy's skin. I knew her in acute ways—her aloneness, her stubbornness, her exalted metaphysics, her sense of destiny. At times the book seemed to know what I was going through at the exact moment of reading. The thoroughness of its investigation was breathtaking, the chastened language tuned to the exact emotional pitch. "I do not know why I am as I am, but I know that my desire to be a woman is so powerful that I can never express it in words. It seems to come from outside of me, for it has much more strength than I have."

I did not have a strong gender identity when I was small. I drew pictures and played with my large family of stuffed animals, to whom I assigned family roles. I read the adventures of the boy reporter Tintin, but I also read the purely quotidian adventures of Martine, a sort of Everygirl, which must have been sent by a relative. I have a distinct but vague memory (I couldn't tell you the year or even the country) of being somewhere with my parents and picking something up—a magazine? a record?—with a girl's face on it, and them laughing at me. I certainly took it as a warning to avoid displaying pictures of girls—to not, say, tack up pictures of Françoise Hardy all over my room, after my paternal aunt and uncle, small-town newsagents, began sending me the French teen magazine *Salut les copains*. But I didn't really know what the laughter meant. Were they laughing because it seemed suspiciously feminine that I would be interested in a girl on a magazine? Or was it because it seemed precociously heterosexual? That second one did not occur to me at the time.

But I was never pushed in any conspicuously masculine direction, either. Despite his interest in sports (he was an avid basketball player in his youth, although five feet, two inches), my father didn't seem to care that I felt no pull in that direction, and we never engaged in the traditional male bonding experiences, not even tossing a ball back and forth. He also never taught me any of his skills: carpentry, plumbing, painting, paperhanging, even shoe repair (he had at one point apprenticed with a cobbler), although that had more to do with class than with gender. The way he saw it, I would grow up to be an important person who would have laborers to do those things for him. He was eager that I extricate myself from the working class and earn my pay from the comfort of a desk chair. He had no objections to my being a writer—he was a frustrated writer himself, who in 1948 had published an O. Henry–like sketch in a newspaper under the byline "Luc Sante."

My mother never taught me her skills, either, not even allowing anyone into the kitchen when she was cooking. But then her mother and her aunt had been legendary cooks and she was forever made to feel like the graceless idiot daughter; her repertoire of dishes was limited to recipes written down by her mother. Naturally she would not have wanted to be observed in her daily race against failure. I'm certain my mother wanted me to be a girl. She struggled with the reality of her stillborn daughter, conflated the two of us, maybe wanted to effect some kind of magical transference.* She feared men, probably with good reason, and would in any case have preferred someone like herself, as much as her girl cousins were like her, someone she could treat with the tenderness her own mother denied her. During our time together, when my father was at work or when we were in Europe and he stayed behind working, I might just as well have been her daughter. I was quiet and timid and serious and cute, with big dark brown eyes, wore a kerchief over my head when it was windy and a little wool bonnet that tied under my chin when it was cold, wore a Peter Pan–collar dickey with my duckling-yellow sweater, and displayed my little knees year-round between short pants and socks.

I can't say with any kind of certainty just when the idea that I might or should be a girl first took hold, but probably it was around age nine or ten. I was an imaginative and fearful child who saw omens everywhere. If I came across a pulp illustration of a note nailed to a tree saying "You will die tonight," I was certain I would die that night. My mother's religion assisted this compulsion powerfully, of course. Any word or act could send one to hell. My mother had put a holy-water font just inside the doorway of my room, and I knew that if I didn't cross myself with the water every time I crossed

---

* She once told me that before I was born, she went to have my sex identified by a man whose father had died before his birth—such people apparently had special powers—who dangled a charm on a chain over her belly, to see whether the ellipse it described was vertical or horizontal. I don't remember her telling me the result. Years later she hotly denied the whole story.

the threshold I would die that night. I was constantly pleading with Jesus not to kill me yet, just as I might ask him for a record player, or a visit to an amusement park, or to spare the lives of my parents if they were late getting back from the store and therefore surely in a car crash, or to prevent my mother from killing me when I got a bad report card. At some point there came the question of the ability of Jesus to turn me into a girl overnight, in my sleep. I don't remember whether Jesus proposed this or if I requested it of him, but there it was, and it wouldn't leave me alone. I trembled, from both desperate wishfulness and naked fear.

I naturally regret my lost girlhood, yearn hopelessly for it, although I'm drawn up short when I actually imagine what being my parents' daughter would have been like, once past age twelve or so. I already chafed under their rules as a boy. My clothes and hair were regulated until I was nearly eighteen. My mother searched my room on any pretext and read every bit of writing she found there. She wanted an account of everywhere I went and everyone I met. She was constantly warning me about bad companions when I obviously had no companions of any sort, all through middle school. But winning a scholarship to a Jesuit high school in New York City was my ticket out of jail. That would not have happened if I had been a girl, and my parents' overprotectiveness would have been in full force for years longer. Would they even have allowed me to go to college out of state? Would I have had to get married to get away from them?

When I was around twelve, the principal of my school, a nun, scheduled a consultation for me with a psychologist. I was going through a difficult period, with no friends and near-daily fights in the schoolyard, serious enough that I dislocated various fingers. The other kids hated that I read books for fun and knew the answers in class; I still had a bit of an accent and was being treated for a stutter by a speech therapist. At my consultation I was shown ink blots, given word associations, made to tell stories about pictures, the usual routine. When I was asked to draw a picture of a man and a woman and tell a story about them, I drew George and Martha Washington and gave a factual account of their lives; I thought that was extremely clever. After the tests, the psychologist asked to speak privately with my parents. Twenty minutes later they stormed out, both of them furious. They wouldn't tell me what they had learned. I just assumed he had told them to ease up on the discipline and allow me more freedom, but who knows? It was right around then that I won the Arbor Day essay contest for my school. There was one winner from each of the schools in town; I was the only boy. When a photo of the five of us was published in the *New Providence Dispatch*, I appeared in the caption as "Lucy Sante."

There were at least ninety-seven things I needed to do immediately to effect my transition, and all of them needed to be done first. I was

winners; Doreen Hahn, first prize for best poster;
nko, second poster winner; and Lucy Sante, es-

immobilized by indecision for a minute. But I'd always daydreamed of going to a transformation salon, to be a girl for a day. I could always have easily accomplished that; such establishments weren't hard to find in New York City. I held back, though, just as I held back on every single opportunity for action I might have taken over the years (e.g., Halloween or glam rock), because I knew that if I took a single step in that direction I wouldn't be coming back. Now that I was ready, however, it was the second or third peak of COVID-19 and everything was closed. I called or emailed every salon between Boston and Philadelphia, but nothing doing.

So I would have to figure out everything for myself. I went online to the female impersonators store, in part because I wasn't sure how sizes worked between the genders. There I was able to buy silicon breast forms, uncanny in weight and texture, and gaffs for flattening the basket. But their clothes were ugly and the wigs were worse. Everything was redolent of a kind of après-disco late '80s suburban glam; everything was shiny and overdesigned. I bought a reddish-brown bob that came down into points, like a helmet for an android ninja lounge dancer, and immediately hated it. I needed regular clothes, so with the usual misgivings I headed for the major online retailer and bought things in large, from underwear and leggings to sweaters and dresses. Some of it looked good and some of it didn't, but it all fit and was comfortable. I took a men's large and was amazed to find that a women's large was almost exactly the same proportions (later I would discover that a women's medium fit me better).

I had always been a clotheshorse, at least since early adolescence. I did, after all, come from a textile town; maybe I inherited some kind of primordial feeling for texture and drape and finish. My father had a range of Harris Tweed jackets and suits, all purchased from the Compagnie Anglaise de Verviers, which offered top-flight clothes at a discount to the workers who processed the wool. He told me how British aristocrats would give their new tweed suits to their groundskeeper to wear for a year or two to break them in, and with that, when I was eighteen, he bequeathed me his good clothes, which no longer had a function in his world. The trousers were too short for me even with the cuffs let all the way down, but the jackets fit me perfectly and I wore them to ribbons. A particular favorite was a gray serge double-breasted number that ended at the hips, 1947 style, just like the one David Bowie wears on the cover of *David Live*.

My passion for clothes got a major boost in 1975 with the appearance of a series of shops, some of them enormous, that sold secondhand or deadstock apparel from the 1950s and early '60s, some of them charging a flat three bucks for anything, from T-shirts to three-piece suits. The Lower East Side had always been full of secondhand shops, and I remember visiting a few when I was a teenager and had no money. In the hippie era they were extravaganzas of Russian military greatcoats and Sergeant Pepper band uniforms and Southern belle crinolines and Congregationalist minister redingotes. These new shops were presciently targeting the style that was still in embryo at CBGB. We all hated 1970s fashion, with its ridiculous tailoring and fire-hazard fabrics and bad-acid colors. We wanted black, which was rare enough that enterprising shopkeepers would keep on hand a rack of clothes they'd dyed black at the laundromat. But on the other hand those old jet-age designs were pretty cool, with unusual prints and color choices and extraordinary textiles—gabardine and mohair and shantung and linen the likes of which I haven't seen since—all of them maybe made for sale at Sears or Robert Hall but with workmanship to rival the luxury brands of today.

In that era I would spend entire days shopping, hours per store, trying things on, comparing items, engaged in learning as much as I was in bargain hunting. I quickly developed firm opinions about collars, shoulders, waists, and ankles. I knew which lengths of coats and jackets worked and which didn't. I could often tell that something was going to fit well just from seeing it on a hanger. I could tell the worth of a jacket from where and how the sleeves were attached and the angle at which its collar sat. I could almost do my shopping by touch alone. I dreamed patterns and colors and designs I hoped I'd someday find, out in the world, since anything could and did turn up in those shops. Not for the last time I had found a seemingly inexhaustible resource in the past.

My passion for clothes fully rivaled my love for poetry, music, and pictures. It was entwined with my love for movies, since every outfit carried some sort of allusion to films of the period when the clothes were new. At the same time my taste for layering drew from the eighteenth century, and some of my standards—for lapels, say—had been formed for all time by the Compagnie Anglaise de Verviers. And there was always a contemporary ragamuffin signal—inevitably I wore something conspicuously torn. They were all men's clothes, but my women friends all wore men's clothes then too. Punk was like certain ceremonial masks from around the world, designed to make the wearer look larger and more threatening. Men's clothes as emphasized by punk were armor, which we figured we needed in the flaming city of the 1970s.

When I finally got the opportunity to shop for women's clothes, in early 2021, I was naturally in heaven. I had come into a bit of walking-around money right about then, which gave me the freedom to make mistakes. And I did, of course. I learned that an empire waist on a long torso will make the wearer look pregnant, that shapeless things like sweatshirts only flatter twenty-year-old bodies, that flouncy tops require considerable mammary buttressing, that puffy shoulders make me look like a linebacker, that suspiciously cheap clothes are best avoided for both moral and aesthetic reasons, that wanting to look like the model in the picture does not constitute a valid reason for buying the garment. I was surprised by how much

I seemed to know already—my subconscious had been taking notes all through the decades—and by how quickly I came to know my own style.

I studied the presentations on the Reddit trans forums and noted common errors. The most frequent was dressing mutton up as lamb, followed closely by dressing strictly for the benefit of the male gaze, often an antiquated male gaze at that. There was also a contingent of persons I collectively named "Mrs. Krushchev," because they favored round-collared sack dresses in loud floral patterns. I sometimes wondered whether those trans women's acquaintance with cis women was limited to frumps and strippers. I felt very fortunate to have my friends: tough, stylish, independent-minded women, some of whom I'd known for over forty years and had seen evolve, who now weren't kids anymore but were not in any way backing down. I modeled my attitude on theirs, and studied their style.

I discovered the lineaments of my repertoire soon enough. Barely a month elapsed between my visit to the female-impersonators store and my trawling for Miyake, Yamamoto, and Comme des Garçons on eBay (the only problem there was the Japanese waist). I found out how much I like cardigans, tunics, three-quarter sleeves, boat necks and scoop necks and V-necks, ribbed tights, dusters, combat boots and ballet slippers, midi- and maxi-length skirts and dresses—I had decided at the very start that I was well past the age for anything shorter. I also recognized how many similarities there were between my male and female styles; my instincts for layering felt exactly the same, for instance. But it didn't seem to me that I was adapting my male style to new conditions. It was as if my male style had itself been put together with a female eye.

Every time I'd go to confession I'd confess the same two sins: disobedience and lying. That dates my trouble with my parents back to an early age, because I don't remember ever confessing to anything else, and just the appearance of the word *disobedience* sets off an audio clip in my head of shouting and screaming. I have a fragment of mental video, in fact, of my going so far as to tell other kids about my troubles, something I didn't generally do. It is fall, and we are standing at the base of the railroad bridge on Summit Avenue in Summit, which means I'm no older than ten. My mother was very controlling, and at some point I began to resist. The funny thing is that while I have vivid physical impressions of our fights, I mostly can't remember what they were about. In sum, though, she laid down the law—all kinds of laws, many of them arbitrary and even counterfactual—and I began to refuse to heel. My mother seemed to have two modes. In one she was tearfully, clingily, cloyingly affectionate, cooing and caressing and kissy-kiss. In the other she was a rattlesnake.

Naturally I can't retrace her evolution over the years with any certainty. I think our trips back to Belgium were peaceful, so maybe something shifted in her after the house was sold and she realized we wouldn't be going back there again. That suggests our relationship began changing when I was about nine, which unluckily coincides with the very dawn of the time when I was just beginning to find new things out in the world (pop music above all) and my own personality slowly began to change as a result. And that was just the run-up to adolescence. Those years, after we moved to a new town (albeit five miles away) where I did not manage to connect with anyone, were massively lonely and unhappy for me. My only recourse was to read a vast amount of literature of every possible kind. My scholarship to Regis at fourteen was entirely unanticipated. The Jesuit high school on the Upper East Side of Manhattan admitted only boys, with no tuition costs—for many years it was funded by the estate of a Tammany mayor—on the basis of a written exam. I'd never heard of the place; the nun who taught me eighth grade suggested it. I got in and my life changed.

I commuted every day, two hours each way, via the Erie Lackawanna Railroad to Hoboken, the PATH train across the Hudson River, and the Lexington Avenue Express uptown. My mother insisted on accompanying me the first three days; the fourth day I felt weightless. Not long thereafter she suffered a breakdown that landed her in the hospital, undergoing shock treatments. I was powerfully disoriented by my visits. Her memory seemed to have regressed every time I came. The first time she thought I was her brother; the second time it was someone more nebulous, maybe an even older layer of memory. At the time I remembered a scene in the movie *The Haunting*, in which a girl ages progressively as she turns the pages of a book. The exact same sequence of events—breakdown, hospital, shock therapy—was to occur again four years later, a month or so after I went away to college. I suppose she felt she was losing another child.

She had wanted a child who would be a replication of her, who would become her sister and eventually her mother. That person would have to worship all my mother's deities, from the Virgin to the king to the little girl, my mother's exact contemporary, to whom the Virgin allegedly appeared just down the road from us in 1933. She had to share my mother's tastes, ambitions, and knowledge of the world and not stray beyond them. If I used a French word she didn't know, my mother would deny that it was a word. (I remember as an adult on several occasions saying "*idiome*" and her hissing back "*idiotisme.*") She feared and reviled anything even slightly hinting at sex. I think she was afraid of her own body. She made me think of those nuns who were said to bathe in the dark so they'd never have to see themselves. She was constantly enjoining me to be *modeste*—that is, to possess a healthy sense of shame, bodily and otherwise. When later on in life I crowed to her about some worldly triumph—my first book or maybe a prize—her entire response was to remind me that he that corrupteth the morals of the young should have a millstone tied to his neck and be thrown off a bridge. In fact we were a lot alike—in temper, judgment, obstinacy, furtiveness, self-doubt, self-pity, self-loathing, in addition to some better qualities—but that only emphasized the ravine-like divisions.

In seventh grade a boy in my class, aiming to provoke, mentioned Allen Ginsberg, the famous bearded poet, "and his boyfriend." The teacher was appropriately outraged, and I immediately went to the public library and found "Howl" in an anthology. At around the same time, religion fell off me, with the sudden mass speed of snow off a tin roof. My piety had reached fever pitch just the previous year, when I went so far as to attend services before school on First Friday and considered making it a daily practice. Now I didn't believe in any of it. Why would an omnipotent and omniscient being get all huffy, and wax his ego, and indulge in petty vengeances, and keep tabs on behavior of strictly local significance? There might well be a creator spirit out there somewhere—who knew?—but religion had obviously been invented by humans, for political reasons. I kept mum, though, in fear that the news would propel my mother around the bend. I would go on keeping up the pretense of regular attendance with her until I was thirty-six, when she found out I was divorced and the jig was up. It didn't cause a breakdown, but a year later she suffered a near-fatal heart attack climbing the stairs to my last Lower East Side apartment.

I think my mother had always slapped me—it was the fashion then—but not with the fury with which she slapped and cuffed me every single day from age thirteen until I left the house five years later. I confess I provoked her. She would poke me, but I would poke back at her until she exploded. She never failed to rise to the bait. With a laugh track it could have been a vaudeville routine, or a sadomasochistic relationship. We spun in a tilt-a-whirl of rage, like two bulldogs in a Tex Avery cartoon. Part of it must have been due to puberty; I was sprouting whiskers and my voice was deepening. She was clearly upset by this, wary as she was of the entire male gender, but tried to salvage things by pushing me into the priesthood, which I was decidedly not having. During one particularly vicious fight she (speaking in house Franglais) called me a "faggot." I was flabbergasted. My father overheard and gently led her into their bedroom and closed the door. Five minutes later she emerged, weeping and shaking, begging my forgiveness. She hadn't had any idea what the word meant. I had to bite my tongue not to burst out laughing.

My father was present for only a fraction of our fights, and often tried to quell them. He also never laid a finger on me, despite my mother often threatening his belt, but he always backed her up. They spoke with one voice; it was impossible to play one off against the other. No matter how outlandish and unpalatable my mother's orders, my father would not countermand them. They never argued in my presence or even that I could hear; I was never privy to any of their serious talk. (As if we were a royal family, I was also forbidden to refer to them by a pronoun; if while addressing my father I called my mother *elle*, she would snap back, "*C'est qui, elle—le chat?*") He drove her to all her religious functions and sat beside her in the pew, agreed to vacation plans that would involve her climbing a set of cathedral steps on her knees, donated funds to a vast array of holy causes that included, for example, the Sacred Heart Auto League of Mississippi, which handed out a magnificent card showing an enormous Jesus resting comfortably on a mountain, watching the cars on the freeway below—even though he himself was at heart an Easter Catholic at best. I got along well with my father, especially when I reached my thirties and had more time and sympathy for him. We could talk for hours.

After his Parkinson's disease evolved into dementia in the late 1990s and he was institutionalized for good, my mother became a somewhat different person for the last few years she had left, no less angry but much less repressed. I could finally see her hidden intelligence emerge. And she was frank, not to say spiteful, about my father. It seems that a female friend of theirs had taught my mother to drive when I was eleven or twelve, but my father had never allowed her to get a license. And one time a tradesman, maybe a plumber, had come by asking for payment, so my mother wrote him a check. When my father came home and found out, he drove to the man's house, ripped up the check, and wrote him another. The checks did bear both their names, but she was never allowed to write one. I was taken aback; I had never seen my father in that light. Their secrecy had occluded any realistic idea I might have had of their relationship. Maybe he was partly to blame for her psychological miseries; maybe they had always been locked in a struggle that I could only detect one side of, owing to his impenetrably reasonable facade. As with so many other things, I would never know.

In early March I joined a local trans support group, meeting on Zoom, where right away I learned a lot of useful practical information, the most important being the name of an excellent local endocrinologist. The meetings varied with the personnel, which shifted almost weekly at times. Many of the participants were very young and worried about coming out to their families or employers or social circles. People went through emotional crises; people got surgeries and we talked them through the pre and post; people would show up on-screen suddenly transformed. One girl spoke so slowly it was as if she were reaching deep into her body to produce each individual word. One person began her transition with genital surgery; only afterward did she begin to take hormones or even present visually as a woman. Some were confident; some were timid; some were tormented; some never seemed to move their heads or bodies or change their expressions for the whole two hours the meetings lasted. Only two or three people of my relative age passed through during the year that I attended.

I corresponded with some friends of friends in other states who were trans; we didn't click. I signed up for a lot of online text-based trans forums. Some of them were dominated by cliques who were continuing conversations they'd been having for years. Others were all about body shaping, or were yoked to small-time specialized commerce, or else there would be a chorus of voices asking: Am I trans? Frequent were the images of outsize bodies squeezed into tiny glittery dresses, with copper-colored polyester wigs worn too low on the forehead. I had been furtively checking out such things ever since I first went online, in 1997. There was a sub-rosa thrill to it then. I wiped the search memory of the shared desktop computer every night, and when I finally got my own laptop I used incognito mode right up until my egg cracked.

I learned about hormones online. I'd heard the term but, being a dunce about science, hadn't realized just what they did. I learned that the range of trans people and experiences was vast beyond my reckoning. I visited endless GeoCities pages, with their primitive formatting, encyclopedic lists of links, and photo galleries that might show twelve minutely different poses for each outfit. I gaped at pages and pages of beautiful trans models from around the world, and was particularly taken with the Japanese otokonoko culture, which had the added allure of seeming impossibly remote. On YouTube I followed the adventures of a group of trans girls in Sydney, Australia, as they finished college, went out for lunch, visited discos, took day trips. I eagerly followed the work of an Argentinean photographer who traveled with a team throughout Latin America to style, make up, costume, and shoot teenagers who wanted to be girls for their *quinceañera*, with results often so spectacular they defied belief—but there the girls were, on video, being girls in the midst of their families, dancing with their grandfather, riding in the limo with their sisters, posing for pictures with the mayor. Could this possibly be a tradition? I felt a sharp pang of envy whenever I saw one of these videos. I always wondered whether they just went back to being boys afterward; I couldn't imagine how that could be.

The internet allowed me for the first time to witness the varieties of transgender experience, to take my time looking, to find the corners of it that appealed and the ones that didn't, to return to pages or videos I particularly liked—although the last of these was not a given, since sometimes people would freak out, renounce everything, and take down their site (temporarily, one assumes). My previous education on the subject of transgenderism had been random, scant, furtive, hasty. I relied on *The Village Voice* and pure chance. I was an innocent, and something of a prude. My early training had been effective at installing in me a powerful auto-repressive mechanism predicated on the fear of being seen. I might *be seen* perusing the pages of that magazine at the newsstand. I might *be seen* entering a showing of *The Queen* (1968). I might *be seen* surveying the displays at any of the seemingly thousands of wig stores in Manhattan in the 1970s. I might *be seen* if I even so much as lurked near Sally's Hideaway or the Edelweiss, never mind going in. And never mind entering one of the drag boutiques or even glancing at their display windows. I might as well have had my own chin in my hand, pointing it out toward the curb.

My absorption of transgender lore before the internet was a matter of seeing things out of the corner of my eye and mentally photographing them, filing them away in the vault marked X. I'd be delighted on finding relevant materials in books or magazines that gave no hint on their covers. For example, I could read at my leisure about the sumptuous gowns, the false breasts, the voluptuous wigs, the cosmetically applied beauty marks favored by various persons assigned male at birth in the court of Louis XV. But aside from such anodyne historical business, my knowledge was as fragmentary as a cargo cult. I now knew there were other people out there in the world who, incredibly, shared my predilections—I had once thought I was the only person in the world who had ever wanted to change genders—but not really much more than that, until the internet.

Even with the flood of knowledge the internet swept in, not to mention the proof it provided of the continuing avidity of my interest, I still managed to deny who I was. That is the riddle I can never quite explain well enough to my cis friends. How can my "egg" have "cracked" sixty-odd years after I first "knew"? The answer is that throughout that time I was engaged in a complex dance of knowledge and denial. Surveying the whole prospect of my life, as I'm doing in these pages, I see how close my trans identity was to the surface in my adolescence and twenties, when I was completely befuddled about it, almost totally ignorant, and had no idea what to do but try to escape it. Then, beginning at the end of my twenties, I switched over into adulthood. The era of adventure was over, my fate had been cast in bronze, and I got married twice, attempting to shove any lingering gender business deep in the crawl space under the stairs, where no one including me would ever see it again. I couldn't really forget about it, of course, but I managed to deny its existence to myself, like a totalitarian state determined to obliterate its past history. Since I couldn't really extinguish the fantasies or the curiosity, I labeled those as perversions I bravely combated. I acted at all times as if other people were peering into my head, inspecting me for faults. I was exercising deniability, and the best way to assure that was to lie to myself. When my egg cracked I simply stopped being able to lie to myself.

But now that I was actually, improbably transitioning, I was impatient with most of what I had found so alluring not long before. I skipped through the various trans forums, maybe dropping a comment here or there but never checking whether anyone replied. I was massively bored with cross-dressers trying on twelve outfits in a hotel room, every picture framing them from the neck down; photographs of people's legs and feet, terminating in kitten heels; forty-minute makeup tutorials involving three shelves' worth of specialized products; long confessions written in some script font with no paragraph breaks and maybe no capital letters; the background music chosen for all transformation videos everywhere. I was looking for things I could use—maybe looking for my tribe. I was always looking for things that felt real: pictures, or moments caught on video, where the staging fell away and people could be seen as just people, however transformed. When I did find those, now and then, they were invariably the work of the young, who were living in a whole new world inaccessible to me.

When puberty reared its head I was entirely unprepared. I knew so little about sex that when a priest—a big Italian who bellowed and told dad jokes—lectured the seventh-grade boys on the facts of life, I was actually learning the major plot points for the first time. The one thing I had learned precociously was masturbation, because back in Belgium, when I was three or four, I had had a set of little plastic cowboys, with bowed legs to snap onto a plastic horse, who twirled a lariat with one hand and with the other grabbed their crotch. Or at least that's exactly what it looked like. I took it into my head to imitate them, and discovered a new kind of pleasure. Inevitably my eagle-eyed mother caught me at it, and for months I was required to keep my hands and arms outside the blanket at night. I had also decided that sleeping with girls was one of life's great goals, although I had no idea what one did in bed beyond kissing and cuddling. When I developed a crush on a girl she became my imaginary playmate, riding beside me in the car, playing with my toys, planning projects with me, snuggling with me under the covers.

I had all sorts of crushes: brief crushes, part-time crushes, subdued crushes, seasonal crushes. Sometimes a girl in my class I'd seen daily for months without really noticing her would suddenly bloom into a crush. And then there was the very occasional megawatt crush, the kind that endured. I was obsessed with Patricia right through fourth and fifth grades, and even though my family moved after that and I never saw her again, I thought about her frequently for many years afterward. She was a slender Irish girl with red hair and high cheekbones and a mouth that curved ever so slightly downward, giving her a bit of a haughty demeanor. I can picture her with reasonable accuracy, but at this remove can't recall much else. I did manage to walk home from school with her a few times—a very bold move for me—but can't imagine what we talked about. I wanted her to be my girlfriend, to cuddle and coo and share experiences, but I somehow also wanted to be her. I would study her demeanor on the way to the Communion railing—the set of her mouth, the hollow of her cheeks, the arch of her brows over her elegantly lowered eyelids—and practiced making my face look that way too. At ten or eleven I perceived no contradiction between those two kinds of desire. On the contrary, I thought she would want me to mirror her—although *thought* doesn't seem like the right word.

I was mostly too shy to speak to my love objects. But then I hardly spoke to anyone at all during the three years of middle school. The genders self-segregated, and I had no friends on the boys' side. I existed far out on the periphery of tween social life, as I almost always had with social worlds. So I was good at being alone. I was never bored, since there seemed to be an unending stream of new interests constantly coming down the highway. I of course wanted to be considered popular in some elevated dream sphere of beautiful people, where I'd relax and my tongue would be loosened. But my schoolmates seemed unknowable—who were they, underneath the affect they all wore like a uniform? I went on a fact-finding mission: an away basketball game, by bus through the snow to Asbury Park. I noticed the tribal division between boys and girls; the agitated horseplay both sides performed; the instances of attempted seduction by verbal abuse; the way the girls remained two steps ahead of the boys in their interplay; how they had to, because all the boys could really do was lunge. I was fascinated. Where did they learn this behavior? Did their parents teach them?

My parents taught me nothing. Nothing negotiable in the social sphere, anyway. My father had long before given up on any kind of social life. He was friendly with some of the guys he worked with, but they were all drinkers, and although no teetotaler, he had no wish to sit in a tavern all night pounding beers. So he watched TV and read and very occasionally went by himself to the driving range. My mother was eager and open, but hampered by her language problems—people genuinely could not understand what she was trying to say half the time. Soon after we moved from Summit to neighboring New Providence, when I was eleven, my parents went to a church dance, and in the small hours invited two couples back to the house for bacon and eggs. Everyone seemed to have a good time, but the other couples never reciprocated or even thanked them, going so far as to avoid my parents at church events. That night marked the beginning and end of my parents' attempt at a conventional middle-class American social life. Afterward my mother fed a pair of old widow ladies on holidays and sometimes snagged some weird foreigner when her tuned ear picked up an accent at the supermarket, but that was it for foot traffic in our house. The rare visitor invariably made me furious; they were a disturbance.

My parents probably would not have been very social even if we'd stayed in Belgium. My mother's social model was rural, encircled, kept largely within the family. She achieved first-name basis with Madame Detiffe across the street—a distant relation, as it happened—but everyone else remained monsieur and madame forever. She was very much afraid of the world, suspecting hidden depths of depravity everywhere. My father had lost most of his friends during the war; his best friend, Fernand, a prisoner of war, was killed during an Allied bombing raid in Germany. My father made one close friend during his time in the Belgian army after the war, a French-speaking Fleming from a ruined bourgeois family, who gave him valuable books and had my parents to dinner with barons and such, but a conclusive rupture occurred at some point not long after my birth, reasons unknown. And then there was Pol Dosquet, our immigration sponsor, with whom he had an angry breakup a few months after we arrived in 1959. A well-meaning Belgian in Summit (not me) brought the two men together around the thirty-seventh year of their feud. They just glared at each other from under their brows like a couple of dogs (*en chiens de faïence*, as we'd say).

One thing I always found interesting about my father: he genuinely liked talking with women. He remained friends with Lucy Dosquet (she and my mother had nothing to say to each other) and maintained an occasional correspondence with the eldest Dosquet, Anna, a well-read spinster. He enjoyed talking and joking with the three rollicking van Hemelrijk sisters—actual aristocrats gone enthusiastically native, who helped us out mightily in the early days—while my mother sat with her hands in her lap and her virtuous half smile pasted on. I enjoyed watching my father at social rituals, dialing up the Maurice Chevalier as he charmed suburban ladies—not that I ever caught a whiff of impropriety, but who knows?

He never talked to me about sex or love or even family life, for all that he could perorate at length about labor ethics, say. My mother of course could only talk about such things with regard to perdition. I hoovered up insane amounts of reading but still didn't know what to read on the subject. I was able to learn about American life through observation, but here I had no such recourse. There was plenty of smut around, but it didn't tell me what I wanted to know. I didn't know whether talking to girls was a difficult science to master, whether there were secrets involved that were shared by everyone but me. And then presto I was off to an all-boys school.

I got along well enough at Regis, but only made a handful of actual friends. The place was not known for producing artists. I did meet new kinds of people: conservatives, libertarians, future priests, prototypical nerds, and, most interestingly to me, kids who were clearly gay, even though the word and its synonyms were never uttered, even after the Stonewall riots happened at the end of our freshman year—but then perfecting Beatrice Lillie impersonations in the lunchroom left little room for doubt. I felt a deep bond of sympathy with the gay kids even if I didn't share their tastes. But my gaydar was nascent—it took a full year or more of intense near-daily correspondence before I finally realized that Robert, my best friend there, was gay. There was nothing effeminate about him, which threw me off; instead he seemed to be striv-

ing for a kind of louche Gig Young playboy affect. We were thrown out of Regis within a semester of each other and now were equidistant from the city in opposite directions, hence the letters.

Before that happened, though, I met Catherine, at one of those extracurricular study groups—on Northern Ireland in this case—designed to bring in girls from selected all-girls high schools nearby. She was both exceptionally pretty and exceptionally intelligent, and somehow we were able to talk together easily, and soon began dating. But she lived in Queens and I lived in New Jersey, so we went to museums and movies and concerts and school dances and never had a chance to be alone together. We had similar interests and similar senses of humor; in our duality she represented the weight of history and tradition—she was becoming deeply invested in the history of painting—while I was all about the new and the moment and the most radical possible opinion on any subject. I must have been barely endurable. (We tried again after college, but by that point our life paths had diverged too much.) Catherine excelled in her role as my introduction to girls. She made me realize that for all the differences of bodies and toilette they were not such daunting and mysterious creatures, but were in fact—all romance aside—much warmer and more engaging than any boys I had known. Not only was it not hard to talk to girls, it was far easier.

But midway through junior year I was sent down. I had failed Greek and Algebra II in the same semester (algebra was just beyond me, Homeric Greek strictly a matter of memorization) and had unexplained absences galore, because I was massively bored with school and in love with the city, in love with the moment, in love with all that qualified as "happening." I just wanted to walk the streets for hours on end, to read in bookstores, to read and scribble in Garment District cafeterias, to take in movies and music all over town, to hang around the hippies on the Lower East Side and figure out what it was they did all day. I didn't care much about my expulsion from Regis—aside from the parental storms I had to endure—but losing my daily time in New York City was the expulsion from Eden. I would be flung back to suburban New Jersey, a well-known wasteland where the present moment was lacking. I imagined my time there would be middle school redux. I braced myself, ready for assault. So it came as no surprise when, on my first day in public high school, as I was walking through the cafeteria, someone said, "Look! He's wearing clodhoppers!" and everybody laughed. But within six months they were all wearing clodhoppers.

I didn't send out that second letter, because Mimi read it and talked me out of it; she thought it sounded like I was pinning the onus on her. But I was writhing in torment, and in an effort to douse the flames actually did send out another letter a day or two later. I accompanied the email with a YouTube clip of Kirsty MacColl covering "You Just Haven't Earned It Yet, Baby" by the Smiths.

> Thank you for your love and concern and patience with me. It's been a hell of a month. I felt like I was being ridden by a loa for at least three weeks of it.
>
> Now I've come somewhat down to earth, or at least squinting distance from it, and I realize that in my metaphysical rapture I've been going way too fast. I need to step it down and I need a lot more counseling. It turns out that my contradictions don't lend themselves easily to binary thinking.
>
> So let's stow the name bit for a while, for example. Yes, Lucy is very much present within me. But I'm

nowhere near knowing how to integrate all the facets into something that will make a whole. I hope that day will come, and soon. In the meantime I have a great deal of work to do, and will be doing that privately.

I appreciate your discretion, as always.

That was not hooey. I was trying to think my way out of an emotional, perhaps existential dilemma. One of the biggest things I learned from the Jesuits was how to put myself on trial and serve simultaneously as prosecutor, defense attorney, judge, jury, bailiff, and an array of witnesses pro and con. I could mount, and demolish with equal ease, a plausible-sounding case on behalf of anything. I had an arsenal of rhetorical weapons that could turn night into day or guns into butter: "that very insistence was a clue to the fragility of my impulse," I wrote in my first attempt. Here, though, I was trying to square the circle. My transition had fully achieved liftoff by then, as impossible to turn around as a Saturn V rocket. But my relationship with Mimi lay in the balance, and my understanding with the entire membership of cisgender womanhood was threatened. So I was trying to talk myself back into the closet.

I'd met Mimi fourteen years earlier, in an online chat group. She was smart and funny and quick and passionately attentive to language and visually alert and endowed with an impressive array of manual skills. I had a full-bore crush on her well before I knew what she even looked like. (In those days before social media I was at length able, after a diligent search, to locate two small, blurry portraits that looked like surveillance photos.) We soon found excuses to write to each other off-site; daily emails became hourly became chats became endless streams of chat. We made each other laugh, traded arcane information, spilled our lives. It was as if we'd always known each other. After three months or so we had to meet. She lived in Philadelphia and I in the Catskills, so we chose neutral ground: Washington Square Park, where I found her eating cherries. Mimi never missed a fruit season.

My marriage was then in its fourteenth year. It had been fraying for quite a while, but a disastrous trip to Europe in the summer of 2006 had finally rent it altogether. My wife and I had simply become incompatible. In 2000 she had insisted we leave the city for good, which broke my heart, and when I had opportunities for us to spend first a year in Rome and then a year in Paris she refused. Cities and Europe were as vital to my happiness as the American countryside was to hers, but she wouldn't share the wheel. I couldn't fight her. And all the tensions multiplied after our son, Raphael, was born, since she had a very specific vision of child-rearing, which I did not quite share. I finally understood its implications when, sometime after our divorce, we sold our house and its ten rustic acres, and she remarked that she was sad because she had envisioned it as the future home of Raphael's generations of descendants. I was flummoxed. The house wasn't much (it was an outwardly striking folk-art version of Second Empire, but inside had been subjected to a soulless 1990s renovation), but more significantly it would never have occurred to me to think of some grand unbroken lineage, let alone that the generations would want to remain in the same place. I completely lacked any sense of family outside the suffocating triad, and my way of being in the world involved living among a density of people.

The day after I came back from meeting Mimi, my wife detected the fact that something had happened, something I maybe gave away through my expressions or body language or possibly scent. I conceded that I had met someone, and she told me to leave. In retrospect I recognize that she wanted me to go off for a few days and ponder my sins and come back chastened, but I took it as final, because for me it was. I stayed in a friend's spare room for a week, and then another friend's trailer, and then took an apartment nearby, since I didn't want to be too far from Raphael. Mimi's visits upstate increased, as did mine to Philadelphia, and a mere few months later we decided to buy a house. I was as happy as I had ever been. Mimi was awfully cute, and life was suddenly fun. We continued to make each other laugh. We enjoyed doing almost anything—the world seemed new and unexplored. I thought we made a good team; we traveled well together. I even liked her family, something that rarely occurred with anyone. And I thought that this time I had finally attained full cisgender heterosexual normality; all my transgender ideation went into mothballs forever, I thought, and continued to think for more than a year.

We naturally had our ups and downs as a couple over time. Mimi grew restive. She was bored in our upstate town, where surprisingly she was not much better at making friends than I was. It was clear that her modest plan to earn money from her art would not work out, since the labor she expended on her stained glass and her prints could have been compensated only with fine-arts prices, and she lacked that sort of market. She felt bursts of painful nostalgia for her freewheeling youth in 1980s and '90s Boston, when people made art for pleasure and disdained all ambition. She suffered intermittent bursts of drama from her extraordinary family, a collection of wildly distinct individuals with a highly approximate collective experience, who had as it were agreed to act as a family. Her parents separated when she was two, and thereafter the four siblings were seldom in one place at one time. Nevertheless Mimi felt her family like it was a part of her body.

We continued to make each other laugh, to act as each other's emotional barometer and referee, to remember for each other, to reliably side with each other in the occasional parish controversies and snipe about whatever malarkey we were exposed to. But cracks had begun to form in the patina. My transgender ideation—which seems as good a word as any for that cloud of whatsits—had for some time been playing havoc with my sex drive, or perhaps I should say that my guilt regarding it was to blame. I could not bear the cognitive dissonance between my love and attraction for her and the dislocation I felt from myself. Worse, I could not talk to Mimi about it, even indirectly. I often set about to tell her that I wanted love but felt paralyzed—but I could not choke the words into forming. She never brought up the subject of sex, either, I assume because she felt hurt. So it lay between us in bed like a young whale.

To ease the awkwardness of coming out to Mimi I relied on a prop. At that time I was taking multitudes of selfies and transforming them on the app. Every day I produced a new favorite, and it was one of these I chose to show Mimi very casually one night after dinner. She had no idea what I was showing her. (Did I expect that she would?) I explained. She was dumbfounded; she hadn't seen it coming at all. But she was immediately warm and understanding. And then whatever emotional surge had made my admission possible quickly collapsed. I did have weird reserves of strength in those days—the gumption required to make all those initial declarations is something I recall with disbelief: the time I lifted a car to save a child. But coming out to Mimi was in a special category, because I suspected it would mean the end of our romantic relationship. I would be immolating my love, and did not really feel I had any choice.

For Mimi the hardest thing was that she had thought she knew me profoundly, just as I thought I knew her, but the person she had invested in had turned out to be not as advertised. On my end I got everything wrong, of course; I misunderstood her position again and again. For instance, I thought it made a difference that I had been concealing my transness not just from her but from everybody in the world, and intended to keep doing so until and even past my death. But I took her point. After all, my major revelation in February was the coherence of the phenomenon, with tendrils that reached into every area of my life. I could no longer pretend that this was a small recurring fetish problem I could keep on ice indefinitely. It was not so much that I had betrayed Mimi's trust, but that I had never honestly earned it. I was naturally staggered by this, and by its implications. Had my entire love life been a lie? I had represented myself as something that I was not. I had been trying to enact the wish I expressed in that song refrain ("If I only have one life . . ."), and as lies will, it had flung itself back at me like a boomerang. I wanted to undo everything, to run the film backward. I wanted to be a regular guy. I wanted to be dead. But at the same time the gigantic momentum of transition had me firmly in its sway despite all pains and misgivings. I would sequester that gear in the closet only for a few days, and I did end up keeping that endocrinologist's appointment, which due to COVID was not for another month and a half anyway.

Soon after we moved from Summit to New Providence, when I was eleven, I was sitting one day in the kitchen, waiting to be picked up by somebody's father for a sleepover back in our old neighborhood. There was a mirror on the table for some reason, and I picked it up and looked at myself. I wore my hair in a modified bowl cut, which needed a trim just then. I gathered the longish loose strands above my temples and bent them into spit curls, wetting them so they'd hold their shape, and brushed down my bangs. I widened my eyes and softened my mouth. I looked just like a girl. Then I heard a footstep upstairs and quickly messed up my hair again. Over the following years that became something I often did on visits to the bathroom: perfecting the doe-eyed look, sucking in my cheeks, parting my lips ever so slightly. Naturally I was studying Françoise Hardy and Marianne Faithfull and Jean Shrimpton. It was around then that my parents finally began trusting me to stay home alone while they went on their endless evenings in shopping centers (entertainment for my mother, as my father trudged behind). So I ventured into my mother's wardrobe, donning her panties, her bra, her slip, her dresses. But never for long. The fact that they were my mother's things had a chilling effect, first of all. And then too, as I was becoming aware of my body odor for the first time, I was certain she would smell me out.

I retreated into fantasy. That required nothing but my imagination, and I had complete deniability. I developed hundreds of scenarios, more or less detailed, some of them refined over many years. Some were single takes: me with my hair in a Dutch-boy bob, say, wearing the girls' school uniform of white blouse, plaid skirt, black knee socks, and Mary Janes. Many, perhaps most, were initiation fantasies. I was eager for the thing to happen, the entirely unanticipated event that I would be powerless to resist, which would conclusively tip me over to the other side. I yearned for this. I would be cast as a girl in a school play and never quite leave off the costume afterward. On my first day of college I would discover that my roommate was just like me, but liberated, with a trunkful of girl things. A wealthy older woman, spotting me on the street, would hire me to be her assistant, but actually as her plaything, whom she would dress up as a fashionable teenage girl and take to society events as well as to bed. I'd meet a girl who would read me immediately and turn me into her girlfriend; we'd go to lesbian bars together and make out. I always set my fantasies in real locations, but my costars were always blurred.

I daydreamed every day and every night, but when I had a crush on a girl I would try to chase out the thoughts; the two things could not coexist. And no one could ever know. I was aware by then that there were others besides me who liked to change genders, but I assumed all the others were perverts. They were fetishists, because that's what this was, a fetish, right? There were men who got off on wearing women's clothes, men who wore ladies' underwear under their male gear, men who liked to play at being French maids or nurses, disgusting old men who liked to wear pinafores and pigtails and sing "On the Good Ship Lollipop" for an audience of their equally senile friends. There was nothing wrong with any of that, of course, nobody got hurt, but it was all just so limited, so superficial, so cheap, so squalid. What made me different—because I always had to be different—was that I actually wanted to *be* a girl, not just look or act like one. But I couldn't quite name that to myself, either. Thinking about actually changing genders was flying too close to the sun. It was physically impossible, I was certain, and of course it was socially taboo, near the top of the degrees of taboo. I simply had to suck it up and pretend I was normal.

That was a bit of a challenge, because I'd never shown any interest in the usual male things. I did subscribe to *Hot Rod* for a year or two in my early teens, but my interest was strictly aesthetic; details about engines put me to sleep. I had no interest in sports or anything competitive, or the pursuit of power and money, or finding my place in the hierarchy through games of dominance and sub-mission, or talking about what guys talked about, especially the way they talked about women. Luckily it was just then that hippie cul-ture was becoming widespread in the white suburbs, and it was okay for boys to wear their hair long and openly declare themselves noncombatants. I came into public high school during a period I dubbed Pax Sativa—it seemed like three-quarters of the student body had started smoking pot, some quite recently, and the craze cut across social divisions. Drugs were a social glue. The lion lay down with the lamb. Segments of the population that might previ-ously have sucker-punched one another during school assemblies now got together and smoked herb in the parking lot of the con-venience store, or in the little patch of woods that hid the nursing home where both my parents were to die thirty years later. All was serene, pretty much. I witnessed no violence during that year and a half.

We consumed everything that came our way, which was primar-ily cannabis of varying strength and pedigree, in the form of weed or hashish. Aside from the very rare line of cocaine produced to great fanfare at an exceptionally important party, and the cough syrup favored by the hard-core—one recent alumnus lined the walls of his room with empty containers of Robitussin, supplied by his mother so that he wouldn't go score heroin in Newark—the rest were psychedelics. I had taken LSD maybe once or twice when I

was at Regis—one time I came home tripping to discover that I had
to spend the evening making conversation with a couple of German
stiffs my mother had dragged in from somewhere—but they must
have been mild doses. In New Jersey we occasionally popped gelatin
capsules of what was called mescaline when we were cruising around
on a weekend night, and all they ever got me was high.

So the first time I took a significant dose of LSD—"Orange Sun-
shine," which by then meant nothing—I was quite unprepared.
When the rush came on it was unmistakably a much more intense
sort of experience than I'd had before, and I immediately started
to panic: the trip would last six or eight hours, a carnival ride I
couldn't exit. And I'd heard the phrase "ego loss" presented as a
good thing, but my ego was all I had—what would be left of me
then? Would I simply dissolve? Had I bought myself a one-way ticket
to the acid-casualty ward? The idea of a one-way ride to ego loss
very naturally introduced the matter of gender, and from then on
the trip was punishing. I had a terrible secret that I couldn't act
upon and couldn't expunge, but that was sucking me in slowly, like
quicksand, as I flailed helplessly. It felt as if I were in danger of conversion to nonbeing, to blue flame, to explosion, to tattered strips
of flesh on the walls and ceiling. And if I survived the trip I was
marked, doomed to lifelong anguish. Thereafter gender dysphoria
regularly came up in my trips and caused me pain and horror. I
knew that my state of mind made me a poor subject for psychedelic

experiences, but that didn't stop me—it was a demonstration of my macho.

In public high school I got along with pretty much everybody. I was book smart but I partied; I hung out heavily but did theater and drew something like an underground comic for the school paper. I didn't really fit into any particular clique, but floated from one to another without major investment. Weirdly I dated only once: a girl so committed to acting like a child I couldn't carry on a conversation with her. Everybody else I liked was taken. But fortunately I met Leslie, and we immediately became friends. That was something completely new: a girl I could simply be friends with, with no particular pheromone activity. She was relaxed and sharp and funny, and she introduced me to her girlfriends. Together they made me feel, no doubt quite unintentionally, like one of them. We'd get together and laugh about others at school, puncturing pretenses, doing imitations with funny voices—I can still hear their various nasalizations of the word *attractive*. It was exhilarating to me, who had never experienced not just female friendship but the comfort of a harmonious group. From then on, wherever I was, I'd always want to hang with the girls, although the option wasn't always available.

In New Jersey I was socially hampered by having no money and no car, in a rich suburb where most others had both. But Bob began picking me up in his MG runabout to go to parties or merely to drive around strange places in northern New Jersey while we got high. I was mystified by Bob's friendship. We didn't have much in common, and I found him impossible to read. He was brusque in his manner and would often lapse into caricatural stoner talk; his entire inscription to me in the yearbook was: "Get yr shit together." I did nothing to encourage him except be needy. I was always half expecting him to ditch me at some tripping party three towns away, but he never did. At his house he'd fling himself into the comfy chair, leaving me the straight-back, and might fix himself a drink twice as tall as mine, but he gave me drugs galore and a great many rides in his two-seater, while I had nothing to give him in return. Did he have a crush on me, or did he simply enjoy my company? I never had any idea. He wasn't much of a reader, but for Christmas he unexpectedly gave me a book, by the English Zen Buddhist Alan Watts, called *The Book: On the Taboo Against Knowing Who You Are*. My reaction was stark terror, which I hoped didn't show. I never read the book.

My friend Barbara Ess was diagnosed with brain cancer in the fall of 2020. I'd known Barbara a bit since the late 1970s, when she'd been in bands—the Static, Y Pants—and put out an ambitious occasional magazine called *Just Another Asshole*. But we really became friends when I started teaching at Bard College in 1999; we were both affiliated with the photography program. I knew and loved Barbara's pinhole-camera photos and her montages, but we didn't talk shop much; we mostly just laughed a lot. I remember a New Year's Eve spent hooting at a biopic of Carl Jung while the other moviegoers looked daggers at us. But when she got sick her devoted students began posting about her on social media, and I realized that I knew nothing of her teaching methods, which were surprising and original. She worked on getting her students to banish all preconceptions, to approach picture-making from point zero, to embrace not knowing; it was all about negative capability, although I don't think she called it that. One student was particularly eloquent in describing Barbara's philosophy and practical guidelines, and I began corresponding with them to find out more. Barbara went critical on the very day my egg cracked; she died March 4, just as I was coming out to my inner circle, of which she would have been part. I felt terrible for having been so caught up in my own drama during her last month.

I watched her funeral a few weeks later over a Zoom link, because COVID was cresting again. The closing invocation was movingly delivered by Leor, the student with whom I'd been corresponding. I'd vaguely known that Leor was trans, but hadn't really registered that fact. Now, seeing her on my laptop screen being passionate, supremely self-confident, wise beyond her years, and quite beautiful, I knew I immediately had to get a conversation going with her on the subject of transition. The following day I invited her to lunch. She did not disappoint. Leor, who chose to keep her Hebrew male name, had a late onset by today's standards. She came out at sixteen and began her medical transition as an undergraduate; she was twenty-four when I met her. She was amazingly comfortable in her own skin, ready to meet the world head-on with no pretenses or apologies. Despite such obvious differences, we were alike in a great many ways.

We developed a routine a couple of months later, when I was beginning to go out in public all accoutered. I'd drive up to Hudson, where she was living, and we'd just walk up and down the main stem for a while and then sit in a coffee shop and talk. Leor's self-confidence was contagious; it was impossible not to feel a surge of pride walking down the street with her. Tourist families would stop and stare at us; older gay men sometimes gave us the hairy eyeball. At first I was conscious of every pair of orbs that lit on me, but gradually I shifted into Leor's unspoken policy of letting the scenery flow by on both sides. Why would I give a toss what strangers thought of me? I began to feel it was okay to be a trans woman, even one as old and imperfectly put together as I was. Leor's lesson, repeated at intervals, made possible my first year of transition. Every time I'd start to think of myself as a freak I'd think of Leor, who was decidedly not a freak.

Besides practical education she also gave me reading lists. As usual I was versed in the past but not the present, so she unrolled for me the panorama of the trans literary scene, which I had not known existed. She was a critical reader, with a sharp eye for cant and preening. She had more tolerance for theory than I did (when I hear the word *theory* I reach for my headphones), but was no one's camp follower. We got a lot of joke mileage out of the "discourse" that neutered every utterance by young persons eager to display their conclusive all-rightness—people groaning under vast heaps of linguistic and behavioral prohibitions they compulsively kept adding to, as if they were Catholics during the Inquisition. I would often completely forget about the forty-three-year age difference between us, because Leor needed nothing explained to her. She was exactly like someone I would have been friends with forty years earlier. She was, when you came down to it, my trans mother—all transsexuals need one. The age reversal fit my golden-age trans puberty.

I made it back to New York City thanks to getting a full ride at Columbia, this despite my having been tossed from Regis and managing to flunk algebra yet again in public school (they gave me an honorary D so I could graduate), not to mention that I was never at any point a diligent student. I had my own interests. The seemingly unmerited scholarship puzzled me for years, until I realized how far down in the rankings Columbia had fallen by then. There were significant campus riots every year from 1968 to 1972, and the school was virtually encircled by a high-crime area. Legacies had stopped sending their kids there; the historically elite fraternities had mostly shut down—one of the houses had become an all-comers crash pad. So they were prepared to take a chance on a weirdo like me, I guess.

I was exhilarated to be back in the city, this time for good, I imagined. But at the same time I was dismayed by the culture of exhaustion I found. By the fall term, 1972, the '60s were definitively over. My first week I attended a meeting of Students for a Democratic Society (SDS), only to have it be the meeting at which the campus chapter dissolved itself. Now the cam-

pus and its surrounds were the stage for competing and sometimes violently warring factions: Maoists; Stalinists from the Progressive Labor Party; ideologues from Youth Against War and Fascism, who might detain you on Campus Walk to check whether you followed the correct line; and the National Caucus of Labor Committees, led by a man named Lyn Marcus, who was really the right-wing cult leader Lyndon LaRouche. One lazy Sunday, looking down at 114th Street from my dorm room, I saw a chair go flying halfway across the tarmac. LaRouche's thugs had just broken up a meeting of independent mayoral candidates being held in the activity center downstairs. Paranoia abounded then; there were cults on every block; conspiracy theories of all stripes and all degrees of insanity attracted adherents prepared to devote their energies to proving them.

To my friends and me this was depressing, but finally it was just noise. For me it was a foretaste of what the rest of the decade was to bring. I would spend it dancing on ruins: the ruins of ideals, of struggles, of the university, of the city, of housing, of transit, of expectations, of ambitions. The system had begun to liberate itself in the previous decade, but choked before it could quite get there. Now it lay broken: murder or suicide? Either way, our inheritance was chaos, which I grew to savor. The city was a vast trash heap of Western civilization, paradise for scavengers like me. A few years later a whole aesthetic grew out of the ruins. It was a transient state of affairs, of course, too precarious to last. One day the big money would see the city as an undervalued property, and then it would be zipped out from under us. For now, though, in 1972, as the white working class shifted its last vestiges out to lawn country, entire neighborhoods lay half-empty, and the props, stagings, and affiliated aspirations of multiple earlier generations were simply allowed to decay where they sat.

Even the McKim, Mead & White campus seemed a bit shop-worn in those days. Anyway, like all first-year students, I was shoved into a recently constructed cinder-block tower on a corner of the property. I may once have fantasized about my future roommate, but what I got was Brian, a burly guy from Buffalo who encouraged the world to see him as Ernest Hemingway—mustache, twinkly eyes, regional accent, elevated ambitions—a modern-day Heming-way with an unmoving helmet of swept-back shoulder-length hair. He was destined to be both a great novelist and a great filmmaker, although I never saw any work by him in either domain. His small talk often involved arcane B movies and their makers. One day he was trying to recall the name of a well-known cinematographer: "That guy with the faggy first name." It was Lucien Ballard, who shared the name with my father. Brian exuded testosterone; it rolled off him in great waves. He and I shared a cinder-block room maybe fifteen by fifteen, with single beds parallel against opposite walls. Night after night I would try to sleep as Brian slayed and conquered, and in the morning I'd hear the kiss-off: "I'll call you sometime." I grasped the concept of microaggression instantly when I first heard the term many years later, because that was the climate in our room, a constant buzz of casually dropped sentences and actions intended to demean smilingly, without actually causing friction.

The cumulative effect was maddening. I was terrified at the thought that the future might just be a long succession of Brians, in every tier of life.

Nevertheless I did begin to find my people at long last. I attended the semester's first meeting of the college literary magazine and met Darryl, who sported a tall Afro, a Fu Manchu, and a cross medallion with bits that hung off the ends of the crossbars so that it rhymed with the Fu Manchu. He told me right away that he was gay, the first time that had ever happened. He was a dentist's son from Indianapolis and heir to a family tradition of "race men," a bon vivant who immediately took me to the Algonquin for drinks, an Anglophile who lined his bookshelves with the many volumes of Virginia Woolf's diaries and letters, a madcap who could whip up entire cabaret routines out of thin air while sauntering down the street after midnight. In every superficial way Darryl and I seemed like opposites—even our lists of favorite books appeared mutually exclusive at first—but really we were siblings, and continued to be over the years.

Through Darryl I met Suzanne, an elegant Francophile with a fashion model's grace, the gravitas of a duchess, a mischievous imagination, and a deep, sorrowing soul. She was going out with Phil, a quick, bright-eyed musician from Ohio, who knew every last bit of arcana about music and baseball, baked cookies when he had access to an oven, and could be counted on for withering opinions.

It would be years before I'd hear any of his own music, and then I'd be amazed. After the midterm break Phil's best friend from high school, Jim, came to check out the campus, and very soon he had transferred from Northwestern. He was a poet with a knack for being forlorn and hilarious at the same time, a gifted mimic and raconteur, a tall guy who hadn't quite yet fully inhabited his tallness, with a great mane of black hair already speckled with gray. He and I understood each other immediately. Our aesthetics aligned, we were both shy and worshipful about girls, and we were poets, which is to say we had tacitly taken a vow of poverty. He didn't tell me he wanted to make movies until years later, when he was accepted by the film school at NYU.

Despite the air of political bitterness and exhaustion that hung over the campus, there were strong new currents blowing in. Second-wave feminism was taking hold, and I was regularly lectured on my behavior. That is, I had to make a strenuous physical and mental effort to break the habits of politesse I had been inculcated with from an early age. If my mind was otherwise occupied I would automatically go on opening doors and pulling out chairs, to the disgust of most of the women I knew. But how different were girls from boys? We ate different things, mostly. Boys ate any kind of slop; girls ate mostly leaves, and if you spent the night at a girl's house there would never be any sugar for your coffee in the morning, maybe honey if you were lucky. But my female friends were all eccentrics anyway, just as much as my male friends. None of us were ever going to actually join anything. We had our beliefs but didn't proselytize, because we were sick of people proselytizing, and for that matter we all basically agreed with one another, so what would be the point?

Gay liberation was happening too, in a big way. After Darryl, a dozen other boys announced to me that they were gay, usually on first meeting. I'd listen to their accounts of the gay dances at Earl Hall and inwardly blanch as they heaped scorn on the one "pathetic drag queen" who turned up. Thanks to Darryl I got a fairly comprehensive view of the Manhattan gay scene, right at the time when it was beginning to evolve into the heavily macho leather aesthetic that ruled up to the coming of the AIDS plague a decade later. The first time I ever went dancing at a discotheque it was at the original Limelight, the one on Sheridan Square that had previously been the nation's first gallery exclusively devoted to photography, hence the name. Now it was a gay club in the old style: open to all genders and persuasions, except cops. Darryl took me and sometimes female friends to Peter Rabbit, on the waterfront, the first place where I noticed the bandanna code; the Loft, the most exalted dance club of its day, where we had to use someone else's name to get in; the Nickel Bar, a pickup joint on Seventy-second Street that brought together young black men and old white men. Late nights would sometimes find us talking and drinking and smoking in nearly deserted gay bars on the Upper West Side, with potted ferns and Gloria Gaynor on the jukebox and Beefaroni in the chafing dish.

Despite everything I remained massively unhappy. My freshman ID card photo shows me looking forty years old, if not fifty, with long greasy hair and an ugly, fitful beard, which I had started growing as soon as my parents finally allowed me to let my hair grow, because hair was a major trigger for me. That year I nursed many hopeless distant crushes. I would decide that girls I liked were too beautiful for me, or too high in station, because Columbia had kicked awake my deeply internalized class anxiety. I was too timid to speak to most of them. I also felt great shame at still being a virgin. It seemed like all the cool kids had been doing it since they were fourteen at the latest, while I'd only barely made out, with just one girl. Nothing happened all first year, but near the beginning of my second I somehow climbed into bed with Claudia, who I never knew at all, before or after. We were both very drunk. What happened then I can only remember in discontinuous flashes. I was sobered up joltingly. I wound up in the emergency room. I hadn't realized I had a condition. I had phimosis, "a congenital narrowing of the opening of the foreskin so that it cannot be retracted." In my attempt at sexual intercourse my glans had swollen to roughly the proportions of a croquet ball. Reading clinical descriptions I now realize that my masturbation technique may well have caused the condition to endure past its usual end at the start of puberty. It may not be coincidental that phimosis is noted as afflicting a disproportionate number of the cases examined by Magnus Hirschfeld in the book *Transvestites* (1910), his pioneering study of gender dysphoria.

I took more acid trips and they continued to go bad from gender freakout. One of them, undertaken with a bunch of random guys from my dorm floor, was pure paranoid psychosis, predicated on the fact that they all knew about my weird secret and were merely biding their time before telling the world. I was profoundly shaken. A few days later I went downtown to a salon for a makeover. Hanging up his towel afterward, the coiffeur invited me to come savor his collection of private movies featuring popular TV stars of the previous decade in their impecunious youth. My hair was now longish and styled, and I had a trim mustache. I could have been a supernumerary on any TV show of the time. I actually looked pretty good, it seems to me now from snapshots, but in the moment I felt I'd been erased—all sides of me—and replaced by, to use a word of the period, a clone. I didn't know whether that was a good thing or a bad thing. I can tell how intense my preoccupation with gender dysphoria was at the time from the number of fantasies I keep archived in the depths of my hippocampus that take place in and around the southwest corner of campus.

Among the images that preyed on me then were the ones of the New York Dolls when they played a show in full drag at Club 82, for decades the city's preeminent drag bar. As a consequence I didn't see the Dolls play until their last days, two or three years later. But I did go alone to see Patti Smith, whom I'd read and read about in the youth-culture press but had never heard. She was playing Le Jardin, a gay disco in the roof garden of the raffish Hotel Diplomat on West Forty-third Street. There really weren't any venues designed for someone like her, because there was no one else at all like her. She hadn't yet put out a record, but I knew in advance, from her poems and her jokes and her attitude, that she was very likely to be the poetry pop star of my dreams. She was all of that, and also rivetingly sexy in an androgynous way I hadn't encountered before. I was instantly in love, and I also wanted to be her. She was funny and charming and inspired and goofy and badass and girlish and daring. This was a girl deeply versed in both Rimbaud and the Marvelettes, just like me. She hadn't really worked on her singing yet, but the roughness only added to its charm. Everything she did seemed as if it had been spontaneously cooked up right then. It was as if my own imagination were being manifested by a much better me. I went home on wings, and immediately, without thinking about it, shaved off my mustache.

By April I was fully into it. I had a complex agenda: things I had to do, read, look up, try, buy, apply. I was a bit frantic, attempting to give myself the entire crash course in one intake of air, apparently. I couldn't help but think of spy movies in which the protagonist radically changes identity from the contents of a suitcase in an anonymous hotel room. I was producer, director, writer, and star. I was building Lucy. It was an amalgam of overlapping construction projects—visual, social, behavioral, internal—that had to be fit in around whatever crazed spurts of nerves or sometimes immobilizing euphoria interrupted their tight schedule. Months before taking hormones I was already manifesting physical changes, or at least so I imagined. I lost over thirty pounds with no effort. I mentioned this miracle weight loss to Mimi, who said, "It wasn't a miracle. You just stopped eating." Did I?

Many of my courses were admittedly brief. I practiced sitting, standing, and moving like a woman for just a few weeks before realizing that my body needed no further prompting. The physical expression I was striving for was exactly what I'd been repressing for so many years. My body already knew all that stuff. I was at last able to shake off the imitation of masculinity I'd worn like a cangue. And then I went further and decreed that if I was a woman, then by definition whatever I thought or did, whatever predilections or prejudices I might have, were perforce feminine. Coincidentally or not, I found myself becoming much more social than I ever had been. I would telephone people—something I previously would have done only in an emergency. I'd be texting and emailing with different people simultaneously—I had only texted with three or four people ever. I realized that this crazy new social energy came less from the gender switch than from the enormous relief of having opened the door and let out all the spooks. I was fresh out of secrets and had no remaining reason not to be completely frank about every subject. I was ready to face the world with all my flaws.

I had rarely worn jewelry—just wedding rings—but now I felt differently about body adornments. So I went to see Barbara, a friend of many years who made exquisite jewelry, eclectic but recognizably hers, and conveniently lived near me. She had made both my wedding rings, one of which I now repurposed, wearing it on my right pinkie. I bought another ring from Barbara to wear alongside it—two of her pieces thirty-four years apart. I also bought a bracelet, earrings, and a leather necklace to which I added a couple of charms, an eye and an inverted cone that made me think of Foucault's pendulum (I've never taken it off). I had dressed up to see Barbara, who lived in a patch of woods up the slope of a mountain. It was my first venture outside the house, but I knew Barbara would be sympathetic. When she suggested we go down to the village for lunch I was ready. I felt wildly conspicuous but people ignored me. Thanks to her I had taken a major step.

The adrenaline rush the experience gave me proved addictive, even though I was shaky. Barbara next took me to a strip-mall Japanese restaurant, followed by a visit to the nail salon next door for a mani-pedi. I had never worn fingernail polish, not even as a rock 'n' roll style, any more than I had ever worn eyeliner. The male employees of the salon were hostile, but then—underpaid and perhaps undocumented—they seemed to be equally hostile to everyone. I did take a brodie when I stepped out onto the humid floor tiles in the rubber thong sandals the shop supplied, but my cover was blown anyway. I was wearing the wrong wig, the wrong dress. I'm sure I looked like Charley's Aunt. But something in me prevailed over such hiccups, and I kept going. I now began to show myself to select friends, mostly at the streamside cabin of the wonderful Annie, always receptive and generous to everyone and the permanent de facto hostess of our crowd. Her house was the most relaxing setting for this difficult operation, which involved my calibrating degrees of response to within a thousandth of an inch, among people I'd in some cases known for nearly fifty years.

My trans support group informed me that because my facial hair had partly gone gray, I couldn't avail myself of laser treatments—which can clear a face in ten sessions but only works with dark hair—but had to resort to electrolysis. With some effort, since the pandemic kept many such places shut, I finally located a widow in a nearby village who had been in the trade for fifty years, working out of the home-office space in her split-level. I'm fairly certain she had never met a trans person, let alone worked on one. And so began a year of painful and expensive weekly visits, the most annoying aspect of which was that I would have to refrain from shaving for three or four days beforehand, since my beard grew so sluggishly— my electrologist began blaming it on the hormones before I even began taking them. I invested in concealer. And since each hair had to be plucked individually and its root cauterized, each session only removed a trifling few. It felt like I was on a hamster wheel, like the process might take me the rest of my life.

Meanwhile, I was teaching a writing course at Bard College, via Zoom for the first two and a half months or so, then in person until the end of the semester. My wisest friend on the faculty had warned me against coming out in the middle of a term, since that would be disruptive, so I worried constantly. I dressed in male clothes and took off my nail polish before every class, except when for some reason I didn't. Would they think it was just a rock 'n' roll affectation? And then I got my ears pierced and had no way to hide the studs. It's a wonder I was able to concentrate on the course matter to any degree. Not that the students would have minded, or probably even cared. But even knowing that, I felt transparent and exposed and in some numinous kind of danger.

But then I began acting in an ambitious student film. For years Kelly, who taught filmmaking, had recommended me to her students who needed a male actor of a certain age, the hardest kind of role to cast, apparently. I appeared in many movies, almost always as a dad or similar figure of masculine authority. It followed from my high school days, when I did a lot of stage acting and, with my precocious beard, was inevitably typecast as the oldest male. In this picture, set in the early twentieth century, I was the mystery man who had left town years before and now had returned from parts unknown. In the climax I dramatically confessed to a murder. I had to be gruff and laconic. My studs didn't work for the part, and I had to take them out and let the skin grow back over the holes, and no nail polish, ever. I enjoyed the feeling that I finally had a secret with an expiration sticker. I enjoyed even more the knowledge that this was my very last masculine performance.

I was approaching the age of twenty and could feel it was a great season of change. During my first year of college I had absorbed the panorama of Western culture as presented by the core curriculum. I fully inhabited the role of student then, eager to master the works of all the names engraved on the pediment of the library. Even outside my requirements I read Freud and Marx and Joyce, attended lectures by visiting greats, attended concerts of serious music, attended gallery openings in SoHo. At one of those I met John Ashbery, and while I was trying to ask him questions about translating Raymond Roussel I realized he was trying to pick me up. I was rattled. It was disconcerting to have moves made on me by my favorite living poet and literary role model, especially since I had dared to approach him with the excuse of a fairly recondite shared interest. At the same time it was a little flattering, since I'm not sure anyone had ever tried to pick me up. (It's entirely possible that it had happened before, while I was oblivious, since I was ever a naïf.) But I had no wish to go along. Poetic or not, maleness did not appeal to me at all, with its acrid musk, its stubble, its needful dangling genitalia, its oafishness and clumsiness, its sense of mission and conquest, its resemblance to the aspects of myself I most despised.

By halfway through my second year of college I was beginning to shift my focus. I became alert to vernacular culture, which in those days could not get past the gates of the academy. I saw movies almost every day; on campus there were usually five or six pictures being screened on any given evening, and not far away were revival theaters and first- and second-run houses of all descriptions. I wanted to write like the movies—as distinct from wanting to write screenplays—so I started reading crime novels; Dashiell Hammett's *Red Harvest* leaped to the top of my canon. I had been a poet all through my teenage years, and in my first year at Columbia had managed to get into Kenneth Koch's poetry class, one of the few writing classes on campus. It was the only class I always attended fully prepared and not stoned; its influence was such that the writing classes I later taught for twenty-seven years were always modeled on it. I learned about style and rhythm from Koch; like

Jacques-Louis David giving his art classes in the Louvre, his primary teaching tool was imitation. I felt as though Koch had pinned poet's wings on my lapel. A year later, in the middle of his course on prosody, it dawned on me that I wasn't a poet at all. I began writing slabs of some kind of prose that was organized like poetry and sounded like a feeble imitation of Dashiell Hammett.

For some months I dated Lisa, a fellow poet, who was very beautiful and completely mystifying. I was mesmerized by her. We stared at each other, played word games, read Gertrude Stein, wrote collaborative poems. I swam in her eyes, which were like the clearing after a storm at sea. For her I went so far as to sacrifice my junior year abroad. I was always susceptible to the grand, foolish romantic gesture, which I never failed to regret. Sure enough, as the semester neared its end I began to think that maybe that hadn't been such a hot idea, as it dawned on me that our emotions were definitely not in sync. The semester before, I had taken a class on surrealism with a recent arrival from Paris, Sylvère Lotringer. I thought it would be a gut, since I had read all the books on surrealism already, but instead it turned out to be an introduction to the French theory that would sweep American academia in the following decades. The material felt chilly, not to say rebarbative, and I understood little of it, but persevered in trying to read Derrida and Lacan. Anyway, I needed to go to Paris, even if I couldn't go for a whole semester, so I signed up for Sylvère's summer program at the house the university owned there.

I paid for the adventure, a whole summer in Europe, with money I had earned the previous summer working in a tool-and-die shop. The machine I ran was an automated multiple drill press, operated by punched paper tape; I only needed to change the piece every twenty minutes. I had all kinds of time, so I read the entirety of Proust's great novel in the Scott Moncrieff translation, figuring that it might be the last opportunity I'd have. I also read Henry Miller's Rosy Crucifixion trilogy, and that led me to Élie Faure's history of art, and with the poetry of Rimbaud and Apollinaire and Desnos already in my head, I was fairly bursting with secondhand Frenchness when I landed at Orly. The city was still very much as it had been when I'd first visited with my mother eleven years earlier: black with soot, perfumed by leaded gasoline, permeated by smoke indoors and out, still vaguely postwar and even vaguely prewar, a place where children played in the streets, where every corner had its bistrot, where every house was ruled by a formidable concierge, where bohemians lived on air in *chambres de bonne*. I was alive to its vibration and wanted to live there forever. Five days after I got there I saw a girl leaning up against a doorway in the Columbia house. She was small, with enormous dark eyes and pouting lips and long, thick, black, wavy hair gathered into a single braid that rode her shoulder, wearing a gray windbreaker and round tortoiseshell glasses. She looked faintly pissed off. I knew immediately she was the one for me.

Her name was Eva and she was a Barnard student from New Jersey, there to take a six-week French-language intensive. She had

a sardonic sense of humor that matched my own. She was in a state of open rebellion against nearly everything. She noticed the same kinds of things that I noticed. We got together immediately and painlessly. We wandered all over the city and into its suburbs, traipsed through picture galleries and geometrically precise parks, wove through markets and arcades, stayed up all night, watched the sun rise over the river, made out profusely in public places, favoring especially the terraces of high-profile cafés. We discovered a shared passion for dancing, in a tiny, barely ventilated African disco in a deep cellar on Rue Saint-André-des-Arts; it was the summer of "Soul Makossa" by Manu Dibango and "That Lady" by the Isley Brothers and "The Payback" by James Brown. We found that we could talk through our bodies, freestyling to each other, thrusting and parrying, exchanging roles, daring each other to top our moves—and that maybe it was more revealing than regular old verbal communication. We had a group of friends we would eat meals with and sometimes go to the movies, but really we were a conspiracy of two, ready to remake the world upside down.

She had a keen sense of the quackeries of language. We developed private codes based on the oracular pronouncements of the autocratic White Russian woman who ruled the house then, and the kumbaya-flavored international-youth-speak practiced at the American Center on Boulevard Raspail. She had an especially good ear for the varieties of English spoken by people who had learned the language later in life, and the accents in which they rendered it. Her father was a Greek immigrant, a psychologist who had been one of Wilhelm Reich's earliest American disciples. When I met Eva, he had recently divorced her mother—a daughter of Greek immigrants, a painter who had been a pupil of Milton Avery—and married a daughter of the German writer Jakob Wassermann, who was a spirit medium; together they founded a pocket-size cult. To Eva's unappeasable rage, the hated stepmother was also named Eva.

I wanted to make love with Eva and knew it was expected and even inevitable, but I put it off for as long as possible. I was terrified. Meeting her was the greatest gift I had ever received, but I was sure I could easily lose her if I failed the test of sex. I had slept with a few women since losing my virginity, and sometimes it hadn't gone so badly as I learned to work around my infirmity, but only relative emotional uninvolvement made that possible. I felt I didn't know what I was doing, that there were explicit rules to sex that I knew nothing about. (It didn't occur to me that if I could take to dancing naturally and immediately, I could apply the exact same energy to sex.) Predictably, my first intimacy with Eva did not go well, although I'm not sure how. All I can remember is her leaving my mansard room at dawn and my staring for hours at the yellow wall. Not long after that she went back to America. I was inconsolable, certain that our relationship was now shattered.

I spent a month and a half traveling around the continent on a

Eurail Pass. I wept over Eva as I sat on a hillside overlooking the city of Bern. In Narvik, at the top of Norway, I danced to James Brown at a disco in a geodesic dome in the August midnight twilight, imagining I was dancing with her, when someone came in with a newspaper announcing Nixon's resignation. In a museum in Basel I saw an exhibition of the works of Lucas Cranach the Elder, hung thematically; I stared for a long while at a row of Lucretias, each stabbing herself through the heart. On a ferry from Denmark to Sweden on which everyone was drunk and almost everybody was at the slot machines, I sat and watched the dancers, all of whom had Down's syndrome, as they clutched and twirled to the music of a trio in red vests. In Rome my youth hostel was in the Olympic stadium built by Mussolini, where the showers only ran cold.

In Malmö, Sweden, I went for a late walk and came upon a hippie porn shop, closed for the night, that had a dense collage of images on its door. Somewhere near the middle was a two-inch-high photo of a pretty young girl with a penis. I was shaken to my core. I could not believe it was a real photograph. How was this possible? Was this person a hermaphrodite? Were there such people in the world? The picture would not answer my questions. In Geneva my youth hostel was in student lodgings at the university, a spacious and well-appointed mid-rise dorm with washing machines in the basement. When I went down to do a load I noticed a heap of women's clothes on top of a machine, cold enough to have been there for a while. Summoning all my daring, I selected a few pieces and went upstairs and put them on. The feeling was exciting and familiar. I went back to put my load in the dryer hoping no one would see me, then returned the clothes thirty minutes later. For many years afterward I had fantasies based on the premise that I didn't return the clothes.

For months I was preoccupied with the matter of my name. I knew perfectly well that my name was Lucy. Over the decades I had occasionally toyed with alternate names. I liked Louise, Betty, Julie, Colette, Simone, Florence; I thought of just dropping my first name in favor of my middle name, Marie. But Lucy stuck. That had nothing to do with Lucy Dosquet or any other Lucys I had met, but went straight back to my appearance as Lucy in a picture-caption typo in a small suburban gazette when I was twelve. The name had taken root in my brain and defeated all comers. That wasn't the problem. What concerned me was my byline. I had been chatting on the phone with Jamie, a painter and filmmaker I had known for more than forty years and who transitioned a few years before me. She told me that her gallery had decided that her work would have to keep being exhibited and sold under the name James, since a mid-career switch would confuse the market. The decision was rescinded a bit later, but before I was aware of that I fretted for months over whether I should do the same. I asked everybody I knew for their opinion. I thought of the strange attributions one sometimes found on detective novels: "John Creasey writing as Michael Halliday." In my notebook I even wrote out a speculative opening for my memoir, should I ever write one: "This book is by Luc Sante, although it was written by Lucy Sante."

I wasn't so much worried about the market and its possible confusion as I was worried about the continuity of my writing, by which I really meant the continuity of my self. A one-letter alteration might at worst make people think the byline belonged to a close relative, maybe. My family name, which does not have an accent and does not mean "health" (it derives from the Walloon for "Alexander"), is extremely rare, and all bearers of it (unless they changed to it from some less wieldy Italian or Polish name) can trace their ancestry back to my hometown. As far as I've been able to determine, I am the only person in the world to bear either my current or my former name. So no one would remain confused for very long.

My own confusion had more to do with the arbitrary line between public and private selves. I published my first professional piece of writing, in *The New York Review of Books,* in 1981, when I was twenty-seven. I had been writing since I was a child, and had published poems and stories in little magazines since my teens, but suddenly being paid for writing was something else again. It was an actual profession, and I had to learn its protocols. My first ten years were an apprenticeship; I published various kinds of literary journalism in magazines and newspapers, and rigorously avoided the word *I*. The act was something of an impersonation. I was playing a character more worldly and sophisticated than I actually was, so I had to keep my real self tightly buttoned up. (When I first began submitting work—fruitlessly—to *Rolling Stone* and other magazines when I was fourteen, I made sure to sign the cover letter "Mr. Luc Sante," so they'd know I was both male and adult.) Naturally I was all but overcome by impostor syndrome. Even when I did start writing about aspects of my life I was careful to keep the rest curtained off.

In the late 1990s I published *The Factory of Facts*, an actual memoir, although I tried to absent myself from the story, or at most to depict myself as a squiggle on an architectural elevation. I wanted to show my whole background, presenting the history of my family, the history of my native town, the history of Belgium, the history of Belgian emigration, and so on—but actually rendering my own face and my own emotions would, I claimed, reduce and standardize the narrative. I thought this demurral was a measure of my seriousness. But of course I was dodging self-depiction because I didn't want to be seen, and I didn't want to be seen because I didn't know who I was. I don't know how much I let myself be aware that the duality of nationalities and cultures mirrored another duality within, but I'm sure I never surmised that metamorphosis would be something I'd experience more than once.

Right up until my egg cracked I continued to maintain the fiction that my writing self was somehow distinct from the rest of me. It went along with the sense I had in my social life that I was always playing a role, the effort of which left me exhausted at the end of every night out. I mostly failed to connect those two phenomena, however, and of course was unable to see what connected them. Somehow or other I managed to avoid considering the possible long-term side effects of carrying around a secret the size of a house. I pretended to myself that what I was trying to conceal was my inferiority to the character I tried to create, in writing and in life. I was boring, clumsy, nebbishy, unsexy, squirrelly, pedantic, useless, feeble, no fun, eternally on the B- or even the C-list of even my best friends. To be sure, this self-portrait was not strictly a by-product of gender dysphoria; my parents' class anxieties, the immigrant experience, and the residue of a Catholic upbringing contributed as well.

My secret poisoned my entire experience of life. There was never a moment when I didn't feel the acute shame of being me, even as I denied to myself that my secret had anything to do with it. I might feel proud of things I'd done, might even be able to summon the will to entertain ambitions, and might ascribe such things to an idealized self I sometimes tried to make myself believe in, but eventually I was going to catch sight of myself in a mirror and that would destroy me for an hour or a day or a week. I've been almost continuously in therapy for thirty-eight years, but because I was guarding my secret even in the therapist's office, no diagnosis ever came close to identifying the cause. At some point in the relatively recent past I came upon a citation from the gnostic gospel of Thomas: "If you bring forth what is within you, what you bring forth will save you. If you do not bring forth what is within you, what you do not bring forth will destroy you." That was an even more effective scare than the line I remembered from William Blake's *Proverbs of Hell*: "Sooner murder an infant in its cradle than nurse unacted desires." It reminded me of the notion popular in the 1960s and '70s that major diseases were caused by festering repression.

It did now and again occur to me that maintaining my secret flew in the face of my commitment to truth and my moral and ethical beliefs. I was actively practicing hypocrisy. At least once or twice I very briefly imagined what it would feel like to open up—I framed it for myself as a career move, just to make the pill go down—but then I quickly iced the thought. Gender transition was the one subject that made me physically uncomfortable. I had no problem with female-to-male transitions, and I could maybe read about Christine Jorgensen or Jan Morris or Renée Richards, safely consigned to the past, but when I thought seriously about my M-to-F contemporaries— Chelsea Manning, the Wachowski sisters, the trans woman who had been a year ahead of me at my all-boys high school and now worked as a pediatrician—I would feel something like vertigo. I'd been afraid of heights my whole life, and this feeling was similar to the sensation of helpless free fall that would clench my gut every time I'd so much as think about height. On one online trans bulletin board twenty years ago I read the story of a Belgian boy whose mother caught him cross-dressing and immediately admonished him to start gender-transition proceedings: "You don't want to be a transvestite when you're forty!" So they had a big farewell-to-maleness party, and the next day she started hormone-replacement therapy. The story filled me with equal parts envy and terror.

What I feared was the one-way trip. I had always known that any exploration of gender I undertook would lack a return ticket, and that is why I had never publicly put on a dress, not even as a joke or a glam-rock fashion statement. Terror of unidirectionality underlay my fear of LSD too; I wasn't so much afraid of the length of trips as of the possibility that they would just keep going and I'd never come back, like the guy in town who swept the parking lot at the diner in exchange for meals and never seemed to look at anything in particular. Unsurprisingly, when I did transition I had the sensation of having passed through a portal. I was troubled by that image— wasn't gender a spectrum? Why did I feel as though I had crossed into another dimension? But eventually I realized that the portal was not between genders. It was the eye of the cognitive needle I had to pass through in order to break out of the prison of denial.

So when I balked at changing my name in professional contexts, I was simply reverting to old habits. I was hedging my bets, making sure I had some way of getting home from the party, ensuring that I had deniability and the option of changing my mind. Similarly, I hung on to various items of male clothing when I enacted my auto-da-fé six months after my egg cracked—not because they were sentimental favorites or possessed historical value but because they represented a phantom back door. It wasn't as if I would ever wear them; I simply needed them for security. For an instant I thought of the man headed for the gallows having his last meal, who saves half his sandwich for later.

As it turned out, Eva hadn't dumped me. She and I inaugurated the fall semester with a seminar on Autobiography in the Nineteenth Century: from Augustine to Rousseau to Mill, Gosse, Carlyle, Ruskin, Cardinal Newman—a fine collection of deep-seated wounds. With fewer than a dozen students, the class also included Lisa, her new boyfriend Chris, and Eva's ex-boyfriend Andrew. It would have made a decent premise for a sitcom. I see Eva sunbathing on the South Lawn, wearing a man's white shirt, a long skirt, and even a big hat, looking like Little Miss Muffett, as she never would again. We went to movies, took drugs, listened to music, went dancing at places Darryl took us to. I got us tickets to see James Brown at the Apollo, but she had a previous commitment so I ended up going alone, memorizing every detail so I could play the show back for her. (What I found surprising was the degree to which the show was pure vaudeville: cartoon, followed by comedian, followed by fashion show, followed by three or four of the secondary vocalists in the Brown company, followed by a full solo set by the J.B.'s, and only then, after more than two hours, did the man appear, and proceed to astound everyone. I could not believe someone could be over forty and fling his body around like that, while also barking, crooning, throwing words like ninja stars, doing the cape routine, giving short homilies, introducing celebrities in the audience. Anyway, at twenty I did think forty was old age.) We got Apollo tickets again a few months later, to see Marvin Gaye, but on the night of were told at the box office that Marvin was sick. They gave us back our $3.75 and we headed downtown, word having belatedly reached us about the existence of CBGB. Patti Smith and Television were playing that night.

Eva, ever the pioneer, realized that the future was downtown, and in the spring of 1975 she took an apartment on Tenth Street east of First Avenue with her younger sister, Magdalen, who was still technically in high school. It was a poor people's neighborhood then, with Polish, Italian, and Ukrainian food stores and old-fashioned haberdasheries and tenements a full construction-standard step down from those in Morningside Heights, and only a few boutiques and record stores remaining from the hippie days just a few years earlier. Eva and I forgot about our classes, pretty much, and spent a lot of time at CBGB and Max's and at a Mafia joint on Third Avenue that featured a six-foot wall-projection TV, blurry with unstable colors, which we deeply loved. We took a lot of black beauties, Eva's drug of choice, and even though they usually made me feel vaguely ill I took them because I loved the comedown, a shivery, ecstatic, continuous series of ripples and chills and occasional quakes of the nervous system. It was something I was to experience again in slightly different form in the early months of my transition, when I thought I was vouchsafed a vision of the divine transgender, although I was not on drugs at the time.

I slid out of school with a huge pile of incompletes. I might have finished eventually had I been able to take a few years off in the middle, since I was so eager to live life, but my parents, who didn't know how things worked, were convinced I'd lose my scholarship if I did that, and no amount of reasoning could change their minds. Anyway I didn't care. I was just as indifferent as I had been to my lottery number for the Vietnam draft, for which I blithely failed to register. I preferred not to. What did upset me was that I had won the Cornell Woolrich literary fellowship, with its stipend of three thousand dollars—enough to live on for most of a year if one played one's cards right—but since its language stipulated the winner had to be a *graduating* senior, I couldn't collect. And then my parents made me go through the cap-and-gown charade for the benefit of the camera and the folks back home. Eva joined us for lunch, wearing her black leather Perfecto jacket over a green silk Chinese dress; my hair was twice as long as hers at that point. She and my parents did not seem as though they belonged in the same movie.

She had cut her hair the year before, the same day we went to see the New York Dolls' *Red Patent Leather* show (visually authored by Malcolm McLaren, all red vinyl and hammers and sickles, a dry run for the Sex Pistols) at a rent-boy bar on Fifty-third Street. She was wearing a shirt covered in tiny mirrors. I was heartbroken. Her hair was a wonder of nature, but she would keep successively shortening it over the years. She was unhappy about being female, which did not prevent her from acting the coquette, not always satirically. She had an analytic mind, a broken emotional gauge, a volatile sense of humor, a severely conceptual imagination, a dancer's body, a goddess's whims. She was a giant ball of contradictions. I loved those contradictions as much as I loved her, but she and they were not always easy to live with. We broke up once, twice; three, four, or five times. If I went a week without seeing her it seemed like a year. But she needed much more out of life than any one being could give her.

She had a thousand projects she was not quite finishing. She would go to diners and order pickles, cottage cheese, and maybe toast. She hated her father, whom I suspected she resembled, and she never let me meet him. She often treated her sister with gratuitous cruelty. She enjoyed reading impenetrable works of philosophy. She was always dragging me down to her grandparents' house, the last Victorian mansion on the ocean in Sea Bright, New Jersey, where her father's orgone box sat in the tower, but when I sat in it I felt nothing. I eventually figured out that she was seeing two other people fairly regularly during her years with me, and probably had side adventures galore. When she lived with me, as she did here and there, and for a whole six months in my apartment on Saint Mark's Place in 1978 to '79, she must have felt stifled and eventually exasperated by my pursuit of the true mystic union. I wanted us to merge into one being, although I may not have thought of it exactly that way in daily life. In any case I wanted to possess her, just as I offered myself to her. But she wasn't having it. She wanted every kind of freedom: no gods, no masters, no jobs, no attachments—not that she didn't love me.

I experienced a previously unsuspected shock when I learned that one of her dalliances was with a woman. I felt like all the air was squeezed out of my lungs. It was one thing to face a male rival, who could have every kind of thing wrong with him, but against a woman I couldn't compete. I did not, of course, probe the significance of this thought. My distress was at its height when we went to a showing of Claude Chabrol's *Les biches*, a gender-inverted version of Patricia Highsmith's *The Talented Mr. Ripley*, expressed as a the-ater of cruelty involving two women and a man. The movie made me feel like a naïf—as many things did—but furthermore made me feel as though love was a charade and the only thing that mat-tered was power. That thought left me first enraged and then in tears I couldn't even explain. I felt that the world wasn't meant for me, that I would always be left out of everything, that as a sexual being I was null.

My last year of college might not have been distinguished by much class attendance, but it was no less a learning experience. I was excited about writing, about all the possibilities offered by prose and genre to someone formed by poetry, who would be getting things wrong in interesting ways. I wrote stories that I published whenever a friend had charge of some little magazine, and with my friends Jim and George planned a magazine of our own. I rounded up contributions from Kathy Acker, Richard Foreman, and Tom Verlaine, in addition to our friends, and art-directed it like a champ, but then George's buddy Larry, who was supposed to print it for us on Physics Department equipment when no one was around, got the yips and screwed us, and we had no money to put it out. Jim and I wore gangster suits, and got our pictures taken in the photobooth at Hubert's Museum on Forty-second Street, and made reading fliers that looked like punk fliers.

With Lisa and her friends we revived the Columbia Poetry Team, which had existed for a while in the late 1960s, and we played Harvard (four people in the seats and our car got towed) and Wesleyan (Jim and I arrived, very stoned and a little drunk, to discover that we were expected for dinner at the president's house; after the reading we were each billeted with a different lovely girl student who offered us her bedroom floor; nothing happened, but neither Jim nor I slept that night). In those days I felt that I owned literature, that I was going to remake it, that I was going to transform the moribund landscape, dominated as it was by people in middle age whom I persisted in picturing as ancient doddering hereditary monarchs. The world was mine to seize.

But once out of school my vision collapsed. To begin with, although I had worked in the library all through my college years, I had given no thought to earning a living. Didn't people just sort of offer you a job when you came out of an Ivy League institution? My father had left school at fourteen to go to work, my mother at sixteen. I only knew about blue-collar jobs and how to get them. It would never have occurred to me to, say, present my credentials to Mr. Shawn at *The New Yorker*; I didn't know you could do that. I had vaguely imagined going to work for a publishing house—scouting out new, bold, revolutionary talent—but when one of my professors got me an appointment with a friend at one of the houses, the first order of business was the typing test, and of course I failed it. Meanwhile my friends were all getting jobs as process servers. It paid well, was filled with interborough travel and the pageantry of life, had no requirements as to grooming or punctuality. So I signed on with the Park Avenue law firm that had hired them, but then the firm discovered that I was a foreign national—an *alien*—and was legally prohibited from serving processes. So I did bank runs and picked up dry-cleaning for a week, with my class rage boiling out of my eyes, until a spot opened at the Strand Bookstore downtown.

The Strand was a cavernous secondhand bookshop, a breakaway success on Broadway from the quietly disintegrating Fourth Avenue booksellers' row, now down to a handful of stores. I wanted to work there because I loved books and had been a Strand customer since high school, but also because it was known to be a happening place; Richard Hell and Tom Verlaine had worked there before going on to fame and fortune. Although I cordially despised the management, the place did not disappoint. Within a couple of weeks I had been anointed head and sole employee of the paperback department. That was not necessarily an honor, since bookmen, as they styled themselves, still considered paperbacks to be trash—although the customers liked them. But for me it was ideal, because anything not bound between cloth covers passed through my hands: garish postwar thrillers, mimeographed poetry journals, multimedia experiments, photographs, maps, original comics pages, girlie magazines of the past, people's diaries and personal correspondence, stamp collections, historic newspapers, an array of business cards that included Muddy Waters's, and once, $550 in cash between the pages of *The Popular Book*.

And yeah, the place was happening. I made friends with Lux Interior during his brief stint there—most of it spent as the store

lookout, his gangly frame perched atop a six-foot ladder in the middle of the floor, ostensibly to spot shoplifters. He was the first person to play me the Sex Pistols, which you couldn't exactly hear on the radio. I witnessed the birth of the Contortions and DNA and Teenage Jesus and the Jerks

and Dark Day, and got to know the extraordinary personalities that populated those bands, almost all of whom pictured themselves as on the run from normal life, like the couple in *Gun Crazy*. Most of my colleagues were gay or women or both, and every last one of us was a weirdo.

I instigated a magazine—we didn't call them zines yet—during the unionization debacle my second year. There was no editor; every contributor paid for their own two hundred copies (we started with three hundred, but that taxed many budgets); and I figured out a way of packaging them. We put out four issues of *Stranded*. In one issue, the senior picker in charge of filling orders from university li-braries, a horizontally expansive figure with the rheumy eyes and general demeanor of a racetrack tout, disclosed his secret identity as Lynne, with a self-portrait in pencil and a poem that concluded: "I am the woman I love," repeated three times. Someone persuaded her to come to a party, a typical drunken punk affair with the music pounding through a guitar amp in a set of sparsely furnished tene-ment rooms, and in she walked, a vision in pink chiffon, with false eyelashes like the ones at the car wash, speaking in a little-girl whis-per. The pathos of the spectacle nearly overcame my ability to iden-tify with it, and fear it.

Naturally I came across all kinds of trans literature in the course of my job. There were popular-science "studies" of this aberrant be-havior, with pictures, as well as "exposés," which were similarly in-clined. I was intrigued, then perplexed, to find a 1932 novel called *A Scarlet Pansy*, by Robert Scully (which I later learned was a pseudo-nym for the 1920s Paris expat writer Robert McAlmon). All the characters were "she" and "her" but didn't think of themselves as women; it was written entirely in camp. When the pansy of the title—a medical student—goes to a drag ball, her costume is her own willowy unclothed form, no more and no less. My problem with it, of course, was that I wanted so badly to be a woman that I could not really understand anyone wanting anything else. Anyway I'm ashamed to say that I disposed of all this literature—which would have considerable monetary value today—by placing it deep down and in the center of the trash bag. In those days they were just paper shopping bags from the supermarket, so street people could and did dig through them. My paranoia, then, extended to the random trash picker, who would have no means of connecting those things to me and even less reason to care. That was also the way I disposed of the beautiful red floral blouse that greeted me when I moved into my apartment, along with sundry poetry chapbooks and punk forty-fives and an autoharp, abandoned by the former tenants, the poet sons of a John Ford actor. The blouse looked really good on me, and I really wanted to keep it, but there was no hiding place deep enough to suit me.

Not long after my egg cracked I began wondering just how it had happened. I knew the mechanics of it, beginning with FaceApp—but what had primed the pump? I began collecting microscopic clues as they occurred to me. It seemed significant, for example, that I had not long before moved four of my favorite stuffed animals from their bag in the attic to the top of my dresser. That kind of display was something I had long avoided. Then there was the fact that the previous autumn I had played Shulamith Firestone in a student movie. All I had to do was wear a long black wig and a pair of plastic glasses and read an excerpt from her teenage diary, but it gave me pleasure. Maybe, too, I was inspired by the then-current streaming series *The Queen's Gambit*, based on the Walter Tevis novel about a girl chess master, with its commanding performance by Anya Taylor-Joy as the prodigy. I identified with it in strange ways, badly wishing to be that character, for all her flaws.

Quite a few of the people I came out to wondered if the coronavirus and lockdown had anything to do with the cracking of my egg. I didn't immediately think so, because I was lucky enough not to be very much affected by it: I have a house, work at home anyway, don't socialize overmuch, and live in a nice town where few people walk, so was able to get regular exercise by hiking all over its far-flung neighborhoods. But then Mimi suggested that my egg might have cracked because I finally felt sufficiently comfortable, and she had a point. We had just enjoyed a very snug year. Mimi had returned after six or seven months of attending to her dying mother and then fixing up her house after she died. It was a relief for her to get away from all the family drama, and it was a relief for me to have her back. We cocooned, as they say, making a garden, cooking, adopting a puppy, entertaining ourselves. Aside from the fact that we weren't having sex, it was as happy a coupledom as I had ever experienced. But would that have been enough to tip the scales?

The most striking feature of my metamorphosis was its absoluteness. The edifice of denial went down as quickly and definitively as the Berlin Wall, and then I started telling people right away. I did not leave myself a back door. My gradually expanding view of how gender dysphoria had permeated my life was breathtaking; there seemed to be no domain unaffected by it. Instances ranged from the tiny and trivial—my discomfort when shirtless, hatred of boxer shorts, avoidance of bodily ornaments—to the major and obvious. There were defenses built to conceal the secret, and other defenses to hide those. I was never at home in my body, did not know what to do with it, was always awkward and clumsy because I could not enter into a rhythm, had to force myself to move, stand, sit in ways that would pass, or at least not draw attention. I had been laughed at often enough as a child. (Thanks to Eva, I came to realize that dancing was a furlough from that jail.)

There was not a second of my life when I wasn't pinned under the klieg lights of self-consciousness. Even when I was alone I was being watched. My mother's shadow was hovering, of course, but I was the one watching me, anticipating all the watchers in school and at work and on the street. I was so good at self-policing I could have saved the taxpayers money. But when I was out in public my preparations were all for naught. There were just too many watchers, and I couldn't properly account for, let alone adjust to suit, every individual point of view I might encounter. This one might think I was too effete but that one might think I was too clerkish. It didn't matter whether the watchers were friends or strangers, people I was attracted to or felt nothing for, long-term acquaintances or people I'd never see again. And all the while I was continuing my immigrant studies in sociology and culture, which meant never letting on that I didn't already know whatever I was just learning—there was that whole other impersonation I was carrying on concurrently. Barring grocery lists, I never wrote anything down that I would have been unwilling to have published. I curated my surroundings as a kind of rebus of cultural signs, displaying faceup those items that would send a message about my judgment and my possession of secret knowledge. Nothing was left to chance in my world, except maybe furniture. I was trying at all times to mount a production titled *Luc*, written and directed and produced by and starring me, as I wanted to be seen, although I never got the impression anyone actually saw me that way.

And I hid out a lot, sometimes spending so long without seeing other people that when I did finally go out into the world again I felt as if I'd forgotten how to talk. In the days before answering machines I'd often put my phone in the refrigerator. Telephones scared me because they were somehow so intimate, also because the ring always sounded like an invasion, also because if you called somebody you could never be sure who would pick up. (My parents didn't get a phone until I was eight. When it rang, which was seldom, it would usually be in the middle of the night, someone calling from Belgium to announce a death.) I was forever claiming that I had no friends, whereas in reality I had at least a dozen people, maybe more, who would have called themselves my friends, and who would have come to my aid if I had asked for it. But I couldn't risk asking for help if I needed it. I had to keep a certain buffer between me and others. When I did socialize I was performing, but couldn't always withstand the rigors of the craft, and when that happened I had to isolate. Very few people ever saw me cry, and I tried to avoid it even when I was alone. (I cried a lot as a child, but on the threshold of adolescence took a vow never to cry again, and kept it up for at least five years.) I realized that sharing feelings with others could be cathartic and helpful, but my secret most of the time blocked the way.

I knew all of this about myself, but did not truly appreciate it until transitioning lifted the veil. Suddenly I could see the entire panorama: the effects of my mother, those of my experiences as an only child and an immigrant, and those of my secret. I had lived in the United States for sixty years by then, and my mother had been in her grave for twenty, so perhaps those influences were weakening. But the weight of my secret could not be underestimated. I could fully measure its effects as they left me. I no longer felt timid; I didn't give a hoot about being judged; I felt like I owned my body, maybe for the first time. So many things about my new being felt familiar, as if I were remembering them. It appeared that transitioning did not involve piling on additional stuff; rather it was a process of removal, dismantling the carapace of maleness that had kept me in its grip for so long. As a trans woman I might now and then feel freakish, or horribly clockable, or out of place, or resented, but those were all projections from without. In and for myself I did not have a speck of doubt. I had once described myself in print as a creature made entirely of doubt, most of it self-doubt, but I had now been given something like a Euclidean proof of an essential truth about me.

By April I was bursting with the need to tell people. I was high atop the pink cloud, that phenomenon known to trans and AA people alike, and filled with missionary zeal. I kept marveling at my own behavior. I had always thought that if by some weird chance I ever found myself transitioning, I'd be slinking around, lurking in the shadows, wearing shapeless clothing to hide my shame. Instead I was pretty much forcing myself on people; I wanted to be *seen*. I sought invitations; I wanted to strut. (I recalled the stunt Peter Cook pulled in the early 1970s, when he dressed up like Garbo and had himself driven around London in an open car while he shouted, "I vant to be alone!" through a bullhorn.) This newfound extroversion did not apply to the supermarket or the lube joint or walking the dog, all of which was potentially hostile territory. But I was fortunate enough to have a fairly significant pool of people who might be on my team, whether out of friendship or human-rights sympathies. So I kept thinking of new people, new crowds, new clusters I could come out to, and when I did I'd send them some version of the letter.

What I was seeking, of course, was affirmation. Despite my ironclad conviction, I still required proof. Hence my 127 daily trips to the mirror, which may have doubled after I started on hormones, to see if anything had changed. And I needed others to mirror me too. One old acquaintance, who herself had begun transitioning until she realized that testosterone was changing her voice—she was a singer—was particularly adept at playing along, flattering, bestowing pet names, giving fashion tips, and generally engaging in campy girl talk (until she withdrew her favors because I wouldn't leap a loyalty hurdle she'd erected). I debated the meaning of gender with Sara for months until we finally agreed it was silly putty. She was virtually the only person I got any sort of pushback from: Why couldn't I just be androgynous? But since she was one of my oldest and dearest, I knew what prompted her reaction and took no offense, and it helped me to talk the matter through with her. Others further out on the rings of acquaintanceship were less helpful. Why don't I shave my head like this beautiful African American twentysomething? Why not cover my cranial nudity with a cloche hat? Maybe I'd like to drive over sometime and pick through a vast collection of secondhand polyester wigs. Maybe I'd like to join this venerable transvestite dining club in midtown. Maybe I'd like to meet their transgender friend who used to be a cop and now lives in the woods.

For years a storefront stood vacant on Avenue A, on its glass door the exhortation LET US BRING OUT THE BEAUTY IN YOU. We were all beautiful in those days, although few of us knew it. There aren't a lot of snapshots from then, because the only people who had cameras were serious about their use. Thus we have a record of the time—Nan's photos and Jim's earliest movies, for example—that is beautiful and deep and chronicles the era's most extraordinary personalities. I wasn't one of those, and my midtwenties were only recorded here and there on the periphery of pictures focused on someone else. None of us have party shots or road-trip pictures or group snaps with people throwing devil horns. By today's standards our lives were very stripped down. We lived in hovels, for the most part, and aside from the inevitable stereo they contained little in the way of current consumer goods; almost everything we owned was secondhand and likely scavenged. That was by both necessity and choice. The apocalypse had already happened and we were living in its ruins, repurposing whatever we found underfoot.

All of us were performing all the time. It was what we had come to New York City to do. Every single person under forty walking down Saint Mark's Place between Second and Third was acting in a movie only they could see. *Band of Outsiders, Expresso Bongo, Ashes and Diamonds, Cruel Story of Youth, Baby Doll, Shock Corridor, Lonesome Cowboys, Night of the Living Dead.* Sometimes you could just about call out the name of the picture when you saw them walk by. And Jamie Nares and Vivienne Dick and Amos Poe and Eric Mitchell made movies about the movies playing in people's heads. We were all about making entrances. Take my gang, for example. With Felice and Alexis at the head we stormed the Mudd Club several times a week back at the beginning, when there was never a crowd and we never had to pay. We were always serious about music and dancing, but the Mudd Club, with its nightclub decor, also allowed you to stage a scene, as Felice once did with stupendous brio. Having just been wronged, she jumped up on the bar and marched down it, finishing everybody's drinks.

Felice and Alexis were old friends of mine from Morningside Heights who had joined the downtown hegira around 1978. When I wasn't at home or at work, I was very likely at Felice's apartment on First Avenue. Alexis was probably there too, and Buddy, often Darryl, Eva when she was around, and Jennifer, a mysterious Antiguan girl who spoke in a rapid-fire South London accent and seemed angry even when she wasn't, plus Fiodhna and Vanessa and Sister Ray from Dublin, Martin from London, and any number of occasionals; Jean-Michel crashed there for a while, until he moved in with Alexis. Felice's stereo was our communal radio station, with all of us at the controls.

There were perennial favorites: "Float On" by the Floaters would get us all up and swooshily pantomiming; Fela's *Zombie* was for when we were feeling nuts. *African Dub Chapter 3* by Joe Gibbs and the Professionals went on like clockwork at a certain hour every day. We marveled and wondered who Poet and the Roots were—it wasn't until later pressings that the artist was identified as Linton Kwesi

Johnson. And when you'd buy a new record you'd take it to Felice's before taking it home. The first spin of the eponymous first single by Public Image Ltd. got us up and leaping—not pogoing, more like stags in the forest. It stayed our anthem for months on end. Another such was "She Is Beyond Good and Evil" by the Pop Group, with its dramatic flicker between disorientation and groove, just our kind of thing. One hot day in late summer, when Felice had just come back from Coxsone's in Brooklyn with a stack of Jamaican twelves, she was leaning on the windowsill taking the air. She looked down at the sidewalk, and suddenly yelled, "Hey, Pop Group! Come up!" So the Pop Group, from Bristol, UK, duly climbed the stairs and joined us for an hour or two of smoking herb and listening to Jamaican twelves. We never saw them again.

Alexis was a parasitologist, working at Rockefeller University. Darryl was beginning to regularly publish critical essays in places like *The New York Review of Books*. Felice was partway through her first novel, a richly detailed canvas of the Detroit of her youth. I remember a spectacular reading she gave from it, probably at Mona's on Avenue A, delivering a sermon in preacherly cadences, punctuated with a white handkerchief in her left fist, shouting like the Holy Ghost was in the room. I, meanwhile, worked in a bookstore and ran a zine that came out about once a year, which seemed to be my only creative outlet. I did make collages then, sometimes band fliers, but I wasn't really writing, just little prose poems here and there. I felt lost. Writing was my only real talent, and I had no idea what to do with it. Sometimes I wrote reviews I intended to submit to *The Village Voice*, but then I'd lose my nerve. And I knew so many serious artists that my little collages seemed trivial. Everybody was starting bands and making Super 8 movies and painting, but I had nothing. I retained a memory of ambition, but not how to activate it. I felt invisible and maybe I was. I met all kinds of cool people at Philippe and Suzanne and George's loft, but when I met some of them again years later, none of them had any memory of me then. The fact that I hadn't accomplished anything prevented me from leaving an image on the photographic plate.

And Eva left me. One morning she sat up in bed and announced she was moving to San Francisco. She had never given a hint of this before, but within a couple of weeks she was gone. She was moving in with Magdalen, who was attending the San Francisco Art Institute and living with one of the singers in the Mutants. I reasoned that since she hadn't specifically said she was leaving me, but only moving to San Francisco, that meant I should move out there too. I immediately quit the Strand and sold the store back at least a quarter of my library. I borrowed some money from my parents and flew west, where I had never been. The sisters and boyfriend were living on skid row—Natoma Street—which in practice meant you kept your car unlocked overnight. The bums meant no harm; they just wanted to sleep in it. In the morning the floor would be covered with empty bottles of Cowboy wine.

Eva and I had sex in that apartment once, but she abruptly stopped in the middle when she said she saw her father's face superimposed on mine. But we hung out anyway. We helped the Mutants shrink-wrap their forty-fives on a machine at Tower Records. We went to a punk party in North Beach where people were actually pogoing and even doing that London thing where dancers wrapped their hands around each other's necks, as in strangulation. We went to the Mabuhay and the Wagon Wheel and hung out with the Zeros from Los Angeles. And Eva and I hitchhiked north one day, wearing our matching three-dollar sharkskin suits from Revenge on Third Avenue, mine in silver and hers in gold. We were headed for Monte Rio, but I don't remember why. (I didn't know until years later that it was the site of Bohemian Grove, where the rich and powerful have been known to disport themselves in drag.) When we jumped off the back of a pickup in some Sonoma County town, the hippies on the courthouse steps all sang the Devo refrain: "Are we not men?" In fact Eva's appearance had grown more assertively masculine over the previous year. She wore strictly butch clothing and her hair in a sort of British public-school boy's cut, long on top with short back and sides (which would become a mainstream lesbian style in the 1990s). One time we were having an argument in the Port Authority Bus Terminal, both of us once again wearing suits, and I could see that every pair of eyes in the waiting room was fixed on us. I looked like a forty-year-old man and she looked like a twelve-year-old boy. What did they imagine?

I flew back to New York alone. She had no intention of coming back, and I didn't really want to stay. San Francisco was beautiful, but it felt provincial and aimless; I needed the world-historical on the daily. I managed to live for four or five months selling to collectors things I'd sold myself at the Strand. It went well for a while, but when I finally scraped bottom and brought the apartment's autoharp over to the Music Inn, the owner handed me ten bucks and suggested I find another line of work. Darryl knew a photographer, Tom Victor, who was looking for an assistant. Tom took portraits of authors for book jackets and magazine stories. He was always tracking down visiting writers to add their faces to his files. One day, leafing through the *Times*, he turned and asked me, "This Knut Hamsun fellow, is he in town?" He was self-taught, and his lighting setups and such were trial and error, something he was shy about even with me; my job was to do billing and run errands. His gift was for charming his subjects and getting them to lower their defenses. He was a nice boss, although I experienced the job as a constant humiliation. I wasn't a writer; instead I was bringing coffee to writers. After six months of it I ran into Noah, whom I'd known since freshman year. He was working in the mailroom at *The New York Review of Books*, where his father was business manager, and there was an opening.

I had disdained that literary world I qualified as "uptown." Darryl sometimes brought me to Elizabeth Hardwick's apartment, where we'd have dinner and get drunk and she'd put on her Billie Holiday records and dance. I loved her, and loved her animated stories of a world that seemed several realms above my head, but I was proud and shy. I hadn't taken her fiction writing class because I'd heard she could be mean and I didn't trust my ability to write fiction. I worked my shaky feelings into a defensive posture—I was downtown and hip and avant-garde and you wouldn't understand. When I started in the mailroom at the *NYRB* it seemed appropriate that I would approach that world as a manual laborer, which is what I remained in my mind anyway. And my relations with the adult world always involved scamming, because I always felt I had to get my own back. Three days a week Noah would have to leave early for his music lessons, so I'd come in about noon; then I'd drag the mailbag to the post office at four and not come back. The job was not a lot of work. I probably put more effort into mailing discarded review copies to my friends.

That was useful because 1980 was the beginning of the major drug years, and I was frequently out of commission for half the day. Drugs then meant cocaine and heroin, sometimes pills like Tuinals, very occasionally opium. I didn't like cocaine very much but I did it anyway. For a couple of years it was as normal as cigarettes. Some friends of mine, very unlikely drug dealers, made their kitchen counter into a coke bar. Everybody would take turns buying rounds for the house, and I might get home before dawn. Once I came over after work, did a few lines, and promptly fell asleep, head on the bar. (I often had inverse reactions to drugs, perhaps because of low blood pressure.) Heroin, though, was just like all the songs say. It was the siren's call, and I was wary of it, making sure to limit my use to once a week. In those days I was buying it from a guy down the hall who was mailed it from Thailand between the pages of books.

That summer Eva came back for a visit, accompanied by her new boyfriend, Eddie. Who the fuck was this Eddie? She'd let her hair grow out for him. He was charming and hard to hate, but I tried anyway. I could not stay away from her. I went down to New Jersey with them and Magdalen, loathing myself for even being there. I wondered whether I was a masochist. But I'd brought some Thai heroin and divided it four ways. It was very strong. I wanted badly to go to sleep, but feared that if I did so I might not wake up. So we wandered through Asbury Park like ghosts, unsteady on our pins, conducting delayed and slurred conversation. At the pachinko machines I won a large pile of small plastic skeletons. In the holy city of Ocean Grove we passed a teenager on his knees, loudly weeping, begging divine forgiveness. Through some kind of inversion the drug seemed to bring physical reality to the manifest unreality of the situation. Or maybe I was dead and everything I was seeing was posthumous. I was distancing the situation in grandiose fashion, making it into a movie, projecting it against the sky of history. I went home and wrote a hectoring prose poem that concluded:

A fuck that comes back the next day is not a culture. History is the phone that rings during the fuck, not the ringing but the duration, the space between. The history of spinning and spinning, and forgetting. It's in the kiss, and you walk it and walk it off and it comes back when it's no longer any use.

In early April I came out to the hundred-member chat group I'd joined at its inception in 2007. It skewed a couple of decades younger and far more academic than my core set of friends, and I had delayed coming out there because—I'm endlessly perverse, no?—there would be no friction of any sort; it would be like jumping out of the window into a tub of marshmallows. Nevertheless the experience turned out to be deeply moving. Alix sent me a heart engraved with my name, which I put on a chain and have never removed from my neck. Mandy made me a bespoke perfume. Veda made me a cloth Lucy medallion with ribbons that looked like a horse-show prize. Chelsey wrote: "The sky out my window literally just brightened." The affectionate responses kept accumulating for a month. I felt like a winner on *Queen for a Day*, a TV game show of my childhood in which women competed for prizes—refrigerators, ranges, vacuum cleaners—by trying to top one another's tales of misery. I sat there on the page as I would on a throne, issuing heart emojis and answering earnest queries. For some reason I decided to share with the group a list I was keeping, scrawled on an index card, of my "role models," by which I meant women who in one way or another inspired or formed me. It didn't take me long to feel embarrassed by this, as if I were tarnishing those women by associating them with me.

There was Françoise Hardy, my idol since age twelve or so. Because I lived in the US, some years passed before I was able to hear her records (many of which are superb, especially when she sings Gainsbourg), so the obsession was totally visual: a beautiful, sexy woman with a touch of the masculine—her strong jaw, her lanky body—and a reserve, bred in the bone, that I recognized as kin to

mine. Patti Smith set off a revolution inside me that began a long process that brought me to this pass. Barbara Epstein was my editor and friend and my greatest teacher, still present within me whenever I write, also a scorching wit and the quickest study ever. Marlene Dietrich I always weirdly but intensely felt I understood; I approved of her fictional decisions as well as the ones she made in real life. It gave me great pleasure to claim the flamboyant French revolutionary Théroigne de Méricourt, whose real, very Walloon name was Anne-Josèphe Terwagne and who came from Marcourt, the village next to my maternal grandfather's—we might be related!

There was Eartha Kitt, indelibly associated in my mind with the term *sex appeal*, like a little picture in the dictionary. Nico functioned for me as a sort of musical alter ego; I played her first four albums again and again during long stretches of my early transition. I inhabited Angie Dickinson as *Police Woman*. Elizabeth Hardwick and Joan Didion both affected my prose for good. Lizzie was another of my great teachers, although I never formally studied with her, while Joan, whom I talked with only once, when we read together at a benefit, was the very model of the disabused eye that I often thought separated us writers from the rest of the population. Juliet Berto was the untamable force in Jacques Rivette's movies: woman as high plains drifter, as all seven samurai, as rebel without a cause. Jeanne Moreau in *Bay of Angels* is who I'd like to be reincarnated as.

There were the French *réaliste* singers, especially Damia and Frehel, who looked at life head-on and whose voices enumerated their scars. I always did identify with Suzanne Pleshette, for whatever subliminal reasons. Ida Lupino's view of the world as a director was already implicit in her acting, and it felt closely related to my own. I wished I could become as perfect and as vulnerable as Mary Tyler Moore. Joan Baez presented the ideal model of how to age well. Musidora's acting walked right off the screen and into the harrowing dreams of its viewers. The list went on like that for quite a bit, name after name: Shirley Clarke, Lotte Lenya, Zora Neale Hurston, Colette, Anna May Wong, Marguerite Duras, Poly Styrene, Thelma Ritter, Emma Goldman, Bernadette Lafont, Isabelle Eberhardt, Memphis Minnie, Jean Rhys, Juliette Greco, Janis Joplin, Lee Miller, Maya Deren, Jay DeFeo, Alice Notley, Brigitte Fontaine, Dorothy Day, Gerda Taro, Gloria Grahame, Bernadette Mayer, Helen Levitt, Billie Holiday, Joni Mitchell.

I felt a kinship with all of them, women who rode alone, in their art or in their lives. They were all women with style and panache that they had created themselves and presented to a world that did not always appreciate it. I felt unworthy of them, I guess, because they had earned their autonomy the hard way, and weren't always able to keep it, while mine had been accorded as a perquisite of having been assigned male at birth. And since so many of them were of earlier generations, when gender dysphoria was not even a concept, I wondered how many would have accepted me as I am. So my embarrassment was not with regard to the people who saw my list, but to the list's members, most of them dead. How mortifying would it be to run into Jeanne Moreau at the supermarket when I was presenting?

I hadn't done that yet, even though everyone was still masked then, an ideal cover that wouldn't always be available. But when the time was right I would know. Transitioning was a budget of paradoxes. I was dead certain but riven with doubts, fearless but liable to be spooked, euphoric but susceptible to sudden crashes, uncertain from day to day of quite what I was doing but somehow following a schedule I apparently hadn't drawn up myself. I would suddenly, from out of nowhere, receive my orders: My hair should be gray. It was time to make an appointment. I should lose the false breasts. I should post my picture on some Reddit forum to see what people say. I needed to get my ears pierced. I had to dispose of another layer of male things. I just thought of another four people to come out to. I needed to get new business cards printed. It was time to have my eyebrows seen to. I would just know such things, and they were to be acted upon straightaway. My mind could be fretting about the opinion of dead artists and whether I actually deserved to join the ranks of women, but some internal mechanism was relentlessly moving the process forward.

In the early 1980s I led two lives. My downtown life was chaotic and reckless. Drugs were ridiculously available and cheap. Just a year or two earlier the dope houses had played games with their customers: making them show track marks, making them wait for unreasonable amounts of time in the cold, whimsically shutting down when there were still forty people in line. Now, though, there were too many dope houses, and competition dictated a reversal of policy. By 1980 you could walk in and buy a bag as if it were a carton of milk. I didn't do that often, though. Mostly I limited myself to free lines from friends when they'd shoot up at my kitchen table after scoring down the street. I was generally strict about it. I wondered all the time how I had acquired this instinct for self-preservation, when I loathed myself and consistently wished I were dead. I was romantically bereft and creatively blocked and always felt like I hadn't been invited to the better party. So why was it other people, who had to be happier than me, who were getting themselves strung out?

I was deeply inhibited, could barely open my mouth unless I was among people I'd known for years. I couldn't make myself step forward. It was as if I were driving a car that refused to go above twenty miles an hour. Quaaludes were popular at the time. My mother had had a prescription circa 1967—I seldom took note of her many drugs, but the name had stuck with me. Quaaludes, a muscle relaxer known abroad as Mandrax, made you sloppy. Once Eva and I made the mistake of going for Indian food after taking some. We had been planning to go to a club afterward, but all our strength went into the digestive process; we crawled home, barely able to stand. But I noticed that the disinhibition quaaludes provoked persisted into the following evening, when one's muscles would be back in order. So I began calculating my dosage, taking the drug the night before big parties. After a while I was taking quaaludes almost every other day. I felt as if I were becoming a different person.

Suddenly I could just call people on the telephone, and I did. I called people I barely knew, on various pretexts. One day, reading about Antonin Artaud's banned radio play, *To Have Done with the Judgment of God*, it occurred to me that there must be a tape of the performance, and I decided to see how many phone calls it would take to locate a copy. (It only took two, and the man whose tape I dubbed, the poet and translator David Rattray, remained a close friend until his death in 1993.) I began to think about performing, from which I'd always felt barred by my inconsequentiality. I badly wanted to sing, but didn't have the confidence to suggest it to my friends in the Del-Byzanteens, and I never had the temperament to take up an instrument myself. Instead I worked up a baroque plan for staging a Grand Guignol version of Thomas Kyd's *The Spanish Tragedy*, its lines stripped down to fit a beat supplied by an onstage dubbed-out rhythm section. I cast myself in the lead, and even designed the costumes, but by then I was scaring myself. I was teetering on some kind of brink. My ideas were getting grandiose (note that I never spoke about my plans with anyone), and the euphoria I experienced increasingly felt like giddiness, on the point of cracking. I had to talk myself down from my high before I did something irreparably stupid.

Those few years were the only time in my life I've ever been remotely promiscuous. I have nothing but fond memories of my *liaisons passagères*, whether with friends or vague acquaintances or people I never saw again, although at the time I denied myself the pleasure because I was fixated on romantic love. There was the Russian woman, staying with friends of mine in a storefront on Tenth Street, who'd come over to my place to take showers, since the storefront had none, and afterward initiate sex as a thank-you. I marveled that sex could be so simple, drama-free, and refreshing. There was the ex-girlfriend of a friend, a worldly, fast-living Italian blonde, who told me that I was an idiot and that I should get circumcised immediately. I'd been dithering for years on the subject, unable to act, but I did it (at the old Cabrini hospital on Nineteenth Street, where you could smoke in the solarium, filled with local characters). There was the beautiful French aristocrat who was in love with death. Years before I ever heard *goth* employed in its present sense, she wore widow's weeds, painted her apartment black, and kept her black drapes drawn; her record collection consisted mostly of requiems. (She did worry me, though. Recently I searched for her online. Her double-barreled name is unmistakable, but accounts of her family make no mention of her.) It really wasn't very hard to get laid then, but I was searching for the Northwest Passage, or the Seven Cities of Gold, or the Ark of the Covenant, or I don't know what. Possibly I was searching for myself.

Around then my crowd began hanging out at a bar called Tin Pan Alley, on Forty-ninth Street off Broadway, across from the Brill Building. The bar was run by Maggie Smith, who reserved the first ten stools for Times Square street people and almost all the jobs for women artists. It was a perfect distillation of my New York, where I could always find someone I knew to hang out with; the jukebox had my two favorite songs of the time ("Totally Wired" by the Fall and "Jah Is I Guiding Star" by Tappa Zukie); John Ahearn and Rigoberto Torres's painted plaster casts of Bronx residents hung on the walls; and you could buy the most diverse items in the men's room. One of the bartenders was a photographer named Nan, a friend of Suzanne's since high school. We hit it off right away and began seeing each other, although the intensity of Nan's social life was beyond my capacity. Her friends always seemed to be in crisis mode, and they called around the clock for her advice and counsel; her phone was the information superhighway as well as a helpline and a confessional. I required a more restful setting, but Nan and I stayed friends anyway.

I was wary of her, though, because I was soon aware of how many transgender people there were in her world. I couldn't even name to myself the terror this produced in me. When Greer Lankton became her roommate, or when Teri Toye showed up at her parties, I hid from them, avoiding all interaction. I was, as ever, in fear of that one inadvertent step that would take me across the line, never to return. That they were actual transgender women made them a singularly dangerous lure and active threat. At the same time, though, I'd have a drink now and then at Slugger Ann's, a bar on Second Avenue, where Jackie Curtis often substituted for her grandmother, the owner. Sometimes Jackie would show up as a woman and sometimes as a man, but in either mode she would turn bartending into a form of theater that was as grand as it was intimate, telling stories and engaging with the clientele. I

loved watching her, although I never opened my mouth except to order a beer. Jackie didn't scare me because she might as well have been onstage, and the place was just a regular working-class neighborhood bar with zero affect.

Years ago, when I was very angry at one of my friends, I pulled down a volume of his diaries and started to read. The joke was on me, though, because the passage I lit on described a night around then, when he and I had gone to see Big Youth at some basement club. Afterward, drunk and high and exploding with frustration at the limitations of my personality, I started kicking garbage cans—the steel kind—off the curb, one after another. (I was mortified to read this, and wondered how many other such performances I'd conveniently wiped from my memory.) I looked forward to making an entrance at the *Times Square Show*, despite feeling rotten that I didn't have any work in it (only a handful of people had ever seen my work), but I drank so many boilermakers beforehand that I zipped through the show and then collapsed on the sidewalk out front, in full view of everyone. (Another decade would elapse before I learned that alcohol would never do me any favors.) But overall my outer life was as festive as my inner life was tormented.

Meanwhile I also had an uptown life. After a year of employment in the *New York Review* mailroom, a job I treated with disdain at best, I was astonished when Barbara Epstein asked me to be her assistant. I could not imagine what had prompted the invitation. I searched my memory for which books I might have been reading at my desk that might have made me look likely—John Reed's *Insurgent Mexico*? Viktor Shklovsky's *Third Factory*? (I somehow forgot that Elizabeth Hardwick was her best friend.) I was entirely unprepared for the job, which involved a great deal of telephoning. I was fine with simple business transactions, but it was harrowing to call the eminent contributors and ask them for their contributors' notes, and as for making restaurant reservations, that was news to me. I'd never, as far as I was aware, eaten at a restaurant that accepted them. I typed with one finger, at my desk in the very center of the

Review office. I was incompetent at every task, except maybe cutting photocopies of the typeset pieces to the width of the column and taping the columns together into ribbons for the layout. It didn't escape my notice that I was a secretary, still very much a woman's job then—I think I was either the first or the second male assistant at the *Review*. I daydreamed about coming to work correctly attired: a sweater, a modest skirt, hose and low heels. I imagined I would have been better at my job.

But Barbara stuck with me, and very gradually our relationship evolved. She became my teacher, in such a subtle way that I didn't at first realize I was being taught. I think she understood my feral aspect, my recalcitrance, my mistrust of the entire adult world, because she recognized such things in herself. (Not long ago Darryl called her an "anarch.") Her teaching began on the level of language, where we both felt most at home. By simply showing me her editorial process and the choices she'd make—the clichés she abjured, the pomposity she deflated, the inapt or inept or inane word choices she altered, the dead prose she enlivened by cutting—she was effectively giving me advanced lessons in writing. Her teaching permanently shaped my work, not by changing it so much as by helping it better be itself. Among the chorus of critics I keep in my head, as W. H. Auden said every writer should do, her voice is by far the strongest and most substantial. She gave me the most important gift I've ever gotten from anyone, shy of life itself: the ability to

arrogate unto myself the authority to speak. It's the reason I can write meaningfully on an array of subjects, without being an expert on any of them; it's the reason I'm able to write this book.

As I came to understand the workings of the *Review*—What was a piece? What was its function? What was expected of it? What were its limits?—I began to think I might be capable of writing for its pages. At the end of another of Eva's visits, in 1981, I accompanied her to Newark airport, feeling glum. To distract myself after she flew off, I bought a copy of *Rolling Stone* at an airport newsstand. On the bus home I read an excerpt from Albert Goldman's biography of Elvis, and saw that it was all innuendo and fake outrage, like a more literate version of a supermarket tabloid. I remembered that Bob Silvers, Barbara's coeditor, had sent the book to three potential reviewers, all of whom had turned it down. I stole the book from the current-titles cart and wrote a review over the weekend. Barbara and Bob accepted it, and with that a new chapter in my life began. It felt to me as though I had been given a career in exchange for Eva.

On May 10, fifteen days before my sixty-seventh birthday, I began weekly subcutaneous injections of Depo-Estradiol, a leading pharmaceutical form of estrogen. My endocrinologist was a warm and understanding young Japanese woman, who did not give me the

third degree, as I had feared, but seemed to accept me and my stupid backstory immediately. Did I want to talk about surgeries? Not
anytime soon, but I would let her know. Did I have any concerns?
No, I was ready to race off the high dive. It took me some time to
master the art of drawing the viscous substance up into the syringe,
and I had to go back for refreshers from the nurses a few times. I was
excited, which didn't help my dexterity. I knew that I would not see
changes for some time, and that they would be glacially incremen-
tal; as the saying goes, "It's not a sprint, but a marathon." Even so, I
was embarked on the journey of my life. It was what I should have
been able to do long before, and at every point in between, but
couldn't. Now that the world had shifted slightly, I was on the moving sidewalk at last. All the objections and hesitations—that I was
too old; that I was dooming myself to loneliness; that I would always
look blatantly transgender; that perhaps I didn't deserve to be a
woman—faded away in the light of my resolve, which came from
that weird certainty. My change of gender seemed fated, as if it had
been prophesized.

I did feel as though estrogen kicked me off my pink cloud, that
the initial thrill was past and I was now about to reenter the world of
adult problems. Then again, looking at my notebook, I notice a slew
of entries from throughout 2021 that describe the same tumble from
on high, again and again. (There are no corresponding entries not-
ing subsequent reascension, but that extraordinary surge continued

to pulse at intervals for another full year.) What was I doing with my time? I was "feeling." I was "transitioning." I wasn't capable of sustained thought or action in any other direction. I took on assignments, almost by reflex, but was unable to complete them. I may as well have experienced a religious conversion or been taken for a ride on a UFO. I was a transformed being, trying to adjust to a new specific gravity, moving a bit haltingly in the newly rarefied air. I was also subject to frequent attacks of dysphoria, which in this instance meant intense gender-related self-doubt, a more acute version of impostor syndrome. I didn't feel any less destined to transition, but felt at those times that I was disastrously bad at it. My friend Pat's Instagram featured a photo, taken in a park somewhere, of a wig atop an upright stick, and I felt an instant shock of recognition.

I was still very much aware of the presence of Luc, whom I sometimes liked to think of as my sad-sack ex-husband. It would happen to me that if I had been writing (I did do *some* work) or had gotten into a conversation about books, say, I would suddenly look up and realize that I felt genderless. And that made sense because my work had always been my refuge from the rest of my life, hence divorced from gender. But at the same time, writing was the arena in which I was most confident, and thus was my claim to, as it were, masculinity. A prerequisite for maleness was that one must dominate at something (belching, sports statistics, blue humor), or at least make an honest stab, and writing was the only field in which I had a shot. In the absence of any other notably masculine qualities, it became the principal signifier of my male identity, and gradually my social personality became coextensive with my work. I was reserved and hard to know, had an endless supply of odd and peripheral information, was capable of a certain dark humor and occasionally handy with the bons mots—my work didn't reflect me; I reflected it. So Luc was in many ways a walking byline. He was an accomplished but deeply unhappy figure, who blamed his unhappiness on all sorts of things: shyness, baldness, solitariness, a lifelong sense of being unloved. He habitually omitted gender from the list. It doesn't answer all the charges, of course, but enough of them.

At one point I wrote in my notebook that transitioning got rid of my neuroses and left me with, in Freud's phrase, ordinary human unhappiness. That may be a slight exaggeration, but it's generally true. The first and most obvious example was the social realm, when I could suddenly, like, just call people on the telephone. It was the second day of quaaludes all over again. I actively needed to talk to people, to surround myself with people, to tell people what was passing through my head. I'm aware that for much of the world this is par for the course, but for me it might as well have been an unforeseen ability to fly. I do believe that my newfound sociability came not from transitioning per se, but from the release of the ten-ton secret that had been stapled to my chest for so many decades. Suddenly having nothing to hide will definitely incline one to weightlessness, and that is a permanent change. When there is nothing left to protect, the result is freedom.

For my birthday party, held in Annie's backyard along the Esopus Creek, I wore a dress, purchased at Target, that looked as if it had been assembled from the flayed carcasses of two or three Indian bedspreads. I also applied too much makeup, badly. I marveled at my effortless daring as I drove to the party, wind in my false hair. I'm sure I looked like hell. It was my first time showing myself to a number of old friends, and it was predictably awkward. I'd been having what I called out-of-body experiences since early adolescence. The first time it happened was my first morning at Boy Scouts camp. I was walking around the main lodge, surrounded by hundreds of boys in olive drab uniforms from all over New Jersey, when I felt an overwhelming sense of dislocation: I was not actually present in the scene, but watching it from across a great expanse of time and space. This sensation recurred every once in a while through the years, usually in situations of major stress or cognitive dissonance; it happened again at the party. It wasn't that everything wasn't lovely, from the weather to the company. I got some wonderful presents, and Mimi made me a cake topped with a large candle in the shape of the number 1. (I thought zero might have been more appropriate, but probably not available at the party store.) But I couldn't yet figure out how to square my various social roles; I would begin a sentence as Lucy and finish it as Luc. I was like a character in a science-fiction novel, trapped between dimensions.

I was becoming an expert on my face. I noticed, for example, that I could look at myself in the mirror and see horror, and then look again two minutes later and see beauty—or vice versa—nothing having happened in the meantime but a change of attitude. I looked distinctly better if I was simply in a good mood, and looked even better if I smiled. Almost everyone who has known me for a few decades has remarked at some point that they never previously saw me showing my teeth in a grin. I had taught myself not to. I thought it made me look exposed, but I can now translate that to read: made me look feminine. I studied photographs of women, all sorts of women, trying to figure out what made a face appear feminine. I focused on the eyes above all. Women's eyes were wide open, reflected light, were directed at someone or something. Men's eyes, by contrast, were most often hooded and unreflective, and often evaded direction, looking at everything and nothing—perhaps an evolutionary adaptation for self-defense. I remembered in my youth thinking, without apparent reference to gender, that my eyes were never sufficiently open. There are scattered snapshots from over the years, beginning around puberty, that show me trying to use my eyebrows to force my eyes open. I'd wind up looking like something you'd try to knock down with a baseball at the fair.

My instincts had seemingly always been feminine. I valued the fineness of my features and couldn't figure out why girls went for guys who looked blocklike or simian or roughly molded in clay. It's not often mentioned that men go through something like a final echo of puberty in their early thirties, when they gain mass in their shoulders and neck and upper arms; this is accompanied by a metabolic slowdown, so that calories are no longer burned at top speed and the pounds pile on. Its effect on me was calamitous. When I went from a 15-inch collar to 16.5—and my waist from 29 to 34 and even 36—I was sure my chance at sex appeal was lost forever. Some important part of me shut down then. At the very same time, blithely unaware of the contradiction, I was trying to look more masculine, which I invariably interpreted to mean looking more severe. I was a broken record on the subject of my baldness, and people tried to console me by telling me how virile it made me look. That didn't help; I thought bald white men looked like pencil erasers. All evidence pointed to the likelihood that I saw myself as a woman, but I could look straight at that evidence and not see it. I was contorting myself in order to fulfill the assignment I'd been given at birth. It was a bad fit, and it had always needed to be exchanged.

In 1982, a full three years after Eva left, I went to California yet again to try to force the question. I went by Greyhound bus, equipped with a three-gram ball of opium I nibbled slowly, which kept me relaxed and dreamy through what otherwise would have

been a three-day blur of discomfort. I didn't nod off until somewhere west of Salt Lake City. I awoke when the bus stopped and
everyone lined up for the exit. We were at a casino in Winnemucca,
Nevada. I stumbled out, barely awake, made for the nearest slot machine, pulled the lever, won the jackpot, filled all my pockets with
quarters, got back on the bus, and went back to sleep. I had won
maybe forty bucks, which didn't much extend the bankroll I already
carried in my jeans, and it was a fool's omen. I ended up staying long
enough in San Francisco that I had to get a job (note that I was on
vacation from the *New York Review* at the time). Eva was working as
an assistant at *PC* magazine, which had not yet begun to publish,
and they hired me as a foot messenger. I was amused by the hippies
who worked there. I had never seen a personal computer. The notion that someday we would all have them seemed pretty dubious,
that they would promote universal peace and harmony strictly delu-
sional. But I enjoyed the job: mastering the streetcar lines, visiting
far-flung neighborhoods, learning about the city's three distinct
weather systems. I revised my earlier assessment of the place: beautiful and well worth spending time in, but a cavalcade of distrac-
tions that precluded it ever being home to someone as serious as I
was, especially now that I was that rare thing, a published author.

I stayed in Eva's large apartment, shared with a roommate, across
from Dolores Park. We mostly just hung out like old buddies. We
would race each other to the telephone every time it rang, because

her number was one digit off from a local movie theater's, and we enjoyed making up funny fake titles when people would call for shows and times. One day, doing the dishes, I found a silver soup spoon with my birth name engraved on the back, one of a set presented to me at my baptism. I was nonplussed—was this a trophy, like a scalp? She disavowed all knowledge. I didn't quite believe her. (The fork too went missing from some collective apartment; it has never been found.) At her job I caught a glimpse of Eva as a functioning adult, agreeable and rational and patient, quite unlike her usual rash, volatile, contrary, bomb-throwing personality; I honestly wasn't sure which I liked better. I suspected, though, that her usual self would soon enough barge back in and disrupt her life again.

The visit has in retrospect taken on a sunset glow of finality, with every remembered item a curtain call. Magdalen was working as receptionist at a phone-sex establishment, a physical office, where young women were posted at desks laid out in rows like so many functionaries. Eva and I went there one sunny day—maybe four desks were occupied; one girl was snapping gum and doing her nails while encouraging her client to see her as his beach bunny—to buy mushrooms from one of the employees, and then we went out to Mile Rocks and communed with the eternal. We went to a new club in the Tenderloin hung with red velvet drapes. It was the summer of "The Message" by Grandmaster Flash. I can still see Eva's small body oscillating and radiating moves outward from its powerful core as she mouthed, "Don't. Push. Me." She was in fact close to the edge. It would be our last dance.

But at the time I was only aware of my own emotions, which combined hurt, loss, diminution, abandonment—the whole cavalcade of my vulnerabilities. I'd known Eva for a bit over eight years, of which we'd been a couple or something like it for five, punctuated by numerous breakups and reconciliations, followed by three years entirely defined by my mulish refusal to let go. Eva liked me well enough, but she did not share my vision of the symbiotic couple, and she certainly wasn't going to be owned. In turn I saw her as completing all my missing parts. She was my muse and in some ways my model; I drew electricity from her. I didn't exactly want to be her— she was, after all, a mess, unable to find her place in the world. She tried on and discarded jobs as if they were coats at the thrift store; took up projects and courses of study she'd drop after a month or two; pondered major changes of scenery, activity, and identity she never got around to acting upon. Nevertheless, in my universe she was the nearest and most powerful star. I was certain that just as she completed me, I was in a position to complete her. She once told me that she got involved with people based on what she could learn from them, a principle that made every kind of sense to me. But I wasn't certain what I could learn from Eva—wit and style, to be sure, although those seemed inextricable from her physical presence. Maybe I admired her capacity for cruelty, as much as I hated being its recipient. Maybe I wanted to hurt others as much as she hurt me.

That is certainly what I seemed to be doing when I took up with her roommate, a sweet, open, rather naive woman from the South, perfectly cast as the unwitting pawn in a *Liaisons dangereuses*–style triangulation. Eva treated her like trash, and when the roommate finally moved out, I moved in with her. I manufactured opportunities for Eva to see us together. I actually had a wonderful time with the roommate, who was genuinely soothing, and not just by contrast. But although our affair clearly irked Eva, it failed to make her jealous to the point of taking action, so I was wasting my time. I got a standby ticket back to New York, out of Oakland early in the morning. The BART trains didn't run overnight, so I hauled out on the last train and spent the night in the airport, reading and dozing, only to find out there were no available seats on the flight. I did that the next night, and the next, and the one after that. After a few days of this I was exhausted, seeing double. I walked in a daze around Oakland, where on a Sunday I couldn't even find a place to buy cigarettes. All the businesses seemed to be concentrated in the lobbies of high-rise office buildings, locked up over the weekend; it seemed like an omen of the future. The roommate and her friends eventually rescued me, took me to sleep in a low-ceilinged house in North Beach that looked as if it might have been built before the 1906 earthquake (recently vacated by the death of its owner, the psychedelic collagist who called himself Sätty), then for a hike up Mount Tamalpais. Thus restored, I called my parents and asked them to buy me a regular plane ticket.

When the taxi pulled up in front of my apartment house on Twelfth Street, I noticed workers on the fire escape, chipping off rust. I knew immediately that the world had changed. My building, a double tenement from the dawn of the twentieth century, was known as the Poets' Building, because Allen Ginsberg and Peter Orlovsky had settled there in 1975, preceded by Larry Fagin and Richard Hell and succeeded by many others. I had gotten in in 1979, thanks to a Strand colleague. My apartment had two bedrooms, a step up from my previous lodgings; that was still a time when you'd move for any slight improvement or salary raise. On the other hand it was on the second floor rear and had no natural light, only a brief burst of reflected sunlight from the air shaft at high noon. Also I wasn't a poet any longer, and felt excluded and resentful, and wore a large chip on my shoulder in all my dealings with Allen and the others. The building was owned by an elderly Polish couple who lived on my floor and had proved incompetent in their management. Not long before I moved in, the tenants had gone on rent strike and won. The result was that the city assigned the building to a receiver, who would settle outstanding debts. When I saw workers on the fire escape that day I knew immediately that the receiver had sold the building behind our backs.

The dark days had begun. I lost count of how many owners the building went through in the course of the 1980s—eight? Nine? Each tenure, characterized by arrogant neglect, prompted a rent strike, followed by endless grinding days in housing court. The city and the neighborhood were changing fast. To my mind, the leading indicator was the Potemkin village known as the East Village art scene, with its eventual 176 galleries (not all of them at the same time). Although I had friends who showed in those galleries and I even came to know some people who ran them, it seemed obvious to me that the mice were deliberately inviting in cats, who would eat them alive, which is exactly what happened. People who for years had displayed themselves on the street as part of the ongoing unnamed local project ("the scene") were now turning pro, looking for the main chance. We had always all dined in the same Ukrainian coffee shops, not complaining about it, but now a new restaurant opened on Avenue A, featuring not-bad Chinese food, sparse decor consisting of small panels from comic books glued randomly on the walls, fluorescent lighting, eighteen-inch-long drinking straws, and a noise level roughly comparable to that of a subway station at rush hour. Annoyance seemed to be the point. Naturally the prices were considerably higher than the neighborhood norm. Around then Jean-Michel disappeared into Annina Nosei's basement and then the cold heaven of fame; I never saw him again.

The first *New York Times* report on AIDS had run in July 1981. Within a year and a half, two people from my building had died— the singer and the manager of the Stimulators—and then the magical Klaus Nomi, who had once appeared at a party I was giving in a borrowed Bowery loft, telling me at the door he was a friend of "Luc and Eva." The toll was to rise consistently year by year until the mid-1990s. The dead included Tom Victor; a dozen former colleagues from the Strand, including Bob Galipeau, my lieutenant on *Stranded*; Martin Davis, who requested that his ashes be scattered on the wooden escalator at Macy's, which happened; and Michael Nash, who taught me everything I know about suavity; my first literary agent, Luis Sanjurjo; Duncan Stalker, the best editor I ever had (after Barbara), and his partner, Met European paintings curator Guy Bauman; my college classmate Howard Brookner, who made the definitive documentary on William Burroughs and would surely have gone on to a major directorial career; my classmates Joe Donovan and Richie Horn, both of them supreme aesthetes; and of course innumerable others. I once saw the claim that my birth year, 1954, bore the single highest toll in the first decade of the plague in

America. I spent some of that time reading to the bedridden and doing their vacuuming, but that's all I could do.

And all the while drugs too were killing people and ending projects and careers; the Del-Byzanteens broke up as a direct consequence. The most unlikely-seeming people were getting themselves strung out. It was as easy as falling down the stairs. At one point in the mid-1980s three-quarters of the people I knew downtown were in detox or rehab. Certain AA meetings became the new VIP rooms, studded with celebrities. Always wondering why I had been spared this particular tribulation, I conducted and participated in interventions, and acted as next of kin for friends in rehab who had no intention of involving their actual families. Abstemiousness became the general rule; cannabis remained a constant, but nothing harder ever appeared among my old crowd again (although there were the inevitable individual relapses). For many years the standard drink at any gathering was a Transfusion—cranberry juice and seltzer—and for many years discourse was littered with AA-speak, which I found annoying mostly when people I was with would stop to lecture mendicants on the street. Self-righteousness was also a feature of the '80s.

In July I decided it was time to reveal myself at my place of employment. I had come out individually to a few colleagues at our friend

Barbara's memorial service a few months earlier, but that made me so nervous that my body had responded by blocking up my left ear, so that I felt dizzy from the disequilibrium and my hearing became even worse than usual; I left sooner than anticipated. Now, better situated, I emailed a short version of the original letter to the president and everyone I knew on the faculty. Almost everyone responded, pleasantly. Quite a few noted that my announcement was "good for Bard." I was charmed to learn that my weird alchemical transfiguration would have a positive effect on the brand. I'll forever be grateful to my colleague Ann Lauterbach, who wrote that it was "exciting to have another great female writer," which is pretty much what I'd been wishing someone would say. I fretted about how to come out to the students. I wrote to various vice presidents and diversity liaisons asking for advice, wondering if there was a protocol in place for such matters. Should I send a blanket email to the student body? Thankfully, someone was sharp enough to point out that they wouldn't read it anyway, and probably wouldn't care. I finally decided to write to the fifteen students in the class I'd be teaching in the fall, maybe a week before classes began. I could wrap it up in about three sentences.

I was presenting during most of my time at home, but bashfully returning to male drag when I went out on errands. I finally persuaded myself that a COVID mask would effectively hide the nasty bits, and ventured forth to the supermarket "as myself," in the lingo of my trans support group. Nobody gave me a second look. It occurred to me that I was unwittingly benefiting from a bad thing: the invisibility of older women. But I was still nervous about walking the dog. I've often said that my neighborhood, in my small Hudson Valley city, was the most diverse I'd ever lived in, including all the ones in New York City. Every race and creed and mode of life was present and accounted for—the gay couple with the bichons frises lived directly across from the extended Pakistani family whose male members wore salwar kameez—and even the whole range of incomes, from the millionaire heir on the avenue to the crack dealer down the street. But we didn't know one another—there weren't any block parties. I'd had pleasant superficial dealings with the neighbors on both sides and directly across, but didn't really know them. Who knew what their attitude might be? It would be months more before I finally ventured out on the street dressed, but by then I'd already shuttled from house to car and back so many times that everyone had seen me and it was no longer a surprise.

In August I decided it was time I spend a few days in New York City. It was absolutely incumbent upon me to walk my life's original catwalk as my newfound self. I had dinner with Darryl, my oldest friend in the city, and his partner, James, at their magnificent house on Mount Morris Park. We had a normal pleasant conversation, as if I had always been Lucy, which was reassuring, if slightly discombobulating when I looked at it from outside the frame. I went to see Jamie, whom I hadn't seen since before her own transition three years earlier. It was very odd to be mirroring each other thus after so many years of denial, although the dynamic between us was otherwise unchanged. We were, after all, the exact same people we'd been forty-three years ago or whenever it was we first met. One of her brushstroke paintings had just been used as the pattern for a dramatic dress by Valentino, so Jamie was in triumphal mode, which for her meant modest and low-key as ever. Then I had dinner outside in Brooklyn with Gary, whom I liked to think of as my guru, because of his accumulated wisdom, always very pertinent, and his matter-of-fact way of expressing it. He had also over the years come to look like a guru, with his long white hair and goatee and a face that at some point during the dozen years I'd known him had deepened into a road map, as if he had still lived under the Texas sun the whole time. I always felt serene around Gary, even out in full view of the public as Lucy.

The next day I was to have brunch with Cynthia and Alexis on the Lower East Side. That presented a challenge, because it was the dog days of summer and my trajectory was across the island, east-northeast from Canal Street, at the widest point of downtown. I didn't want to call a car and it was impossible to hail a regular cab in the permanent tunnel jam, so I had to hoof it in the sweltering heat. My wig, which had taken two months to arrive from China and was advertised as some superior grade of "virgin" hair, turned into a mass of straw. The wise women at Love Hair, my local wig salon, had advised me that it was synthetic, but I had invested too much to want to believe them. Meanwhile my dress, bought cheap online and of some jersey-like material, turned out not to breathe. It was a convection oven. And the whole way as I sweated I felt stared at by the entire population of New York City. It was lovely seeing my friends, who were kind and soothing, but I felt ugly and foolish and a cheap impostor. I slunk home wigless in a T-shirt and shorts and threw wig and dress in the trash the minute I got there.

It was a paradox: at home I was wary of the population but felt myself beyond criticism however I was presenting, whereas in the city I felt safe, but a sorry public spectacle. Anyway my alternate wig cost a third what the first one had and arrived almost instantly from the major online retailer. I thought it was synthetic, but the Love Hair ladies assured me it was real, and as usual they were right; it just needed a wash. It became my permanent hair. It is in fact so central an aspect of me that now and then I lapse into brooding about authenticity. How can I be defined by something I didn't grow or make? Well, some people have alopecia or cancer; some have religious proscriptions; some people's image is centered around their suits or their glasses or their tattoos; some people just wear wigs all the time for fun. Angelika, my German friend in Belgium, suggested that I might get a hair transplant in Turkey. It's evidently what all the German politicians do, and there are some surprisingly low-cost flight-hotel-surgery packages. I'd always wanted to visit

Istanbul, but I also considered that my hair had never been much of a bargain to begin with. It tended toward lank and lifeless. All I knew how to do as a teenager was to wash it with baby shampoo, dry it to a frizz with a towel, and then not brush it; it still looked awful. I made my peace with the wig, which had anyway come to feel like a part of my body.

I was just beginning to wake up in the morning knowing who I was. For months I'd awakened in a gray interzone, somewhere between genders and perhaps between realities. It reminded me of the interval between languages I'd had to pass through every day when I was first learning English. In fact there was a distinct rhyme between gender transition and the sort of transitioning I'd had to do as an immigrant child becoming acculturated in the United States. Both involved rapid, total, full-body education, at once accumulating tiny details and apprehending gestalt. My textbooks were everywhere, especially on the street. A few minor disasters aside, I didn't feel self-conscious as much as I felt conscious, period. I made no special effort to alter my movement or behavior, but on the other hand there were new social boundaries I had to observe. I'd always been curious about people and had always calmly observed those around me—on the subway, say. But I couldn't do that anymore, because as a woman I would be inviting unwanted attention. The single greatest perquisite of maleness, for me, had been a certain invisibility. To be sure, it had its roots in self-loathing, but it was tremendously useful in navigating public spaces, especially in unfamiliar if not outright hostile neighborhoods and foreign cities. And the sense worked best at night; I'd always been a night walker. But that was now gone. My invisibility as an older woman did not extend to certain areas after dark. I would have to watch where I went and when and how.

My identity was to some degree in flux, and would likely be for years to come. There were certain habits of thought that had become rooted after sixty-odd years. I was constantly misgendering myself internally—I hadn't previously been aware of just how much third-person narration accompanied my every action, in some semiconscious lower register. That was presumably a vestige of childhood, when I cast myself as the protagonist of an internal cinema that dramatized dull reality. And nearly every day at some point I'd find myself overcome by sheer incredulity, that I had actually gone and done this thing that had haunted me all my life and that I had been so invested in suppressing. It was as if I'd been struck by lightning, or rescued from a cave-in, or returned from a near-death experience. I had been liberated—by mysterious forces, it often seemed—and my immediate task was to relearn normal life under vastly changed conditions.

Meanwhile my body was doing things. One day I accidentally slammed the swing door in the kitchen on myself, and caught the impact full in the chest, which taught me about a brand-new kind of pain. Before long I had breasts the size of eggs, then the size of oranges. My skin had become extraordinarily soft, and the hair on my hands and arms disappeared, followed later by that on my chest and legs. I lost muscle mass in my shoulders and upper arms, and my natural waist asserted itself. Was my ass getting bigger? I had a hard time telling. My face was changing incrementally. My chin actually appeared to shrink; my eyes, the bellwether, became more alert. I wrote in my notebook—and then discovered I'd written it twice in the space of a month—that my face was like the duck-rabbit optical illusion. You could see it as male or as female, depending on your expectations. The balance seemed to gradually tip more toward the F over time, although I'd likely be aware of the M until the end of my life, even if I took estrogen the whole way. But anyway I began to feel plausible, at least on some days.

My youth ended early in 1983, before my twenty-ninth birthday. It was a tiered succession of events, like cascading organ failure. Doors had been closing for some time, and, it's true, a few opened for me, such as the possibility of writing for a living. On my thirtieth birthday, a year later, I quit *The New York Review of Books* to launch myself into the wild blue, and I never worked a forty-hour week outside my house again. But overall that time felt like the ringing down of a steel curtain, the shuttering of a domain in which I should have made something of myself, but didn't. This new time felt all wrong: all the money display everywhere; the advent of the restaurants; the circus-like parties; the Absolut ads and Macintosh ads and Johnnie Walker Red ads that brought downtown celebutantes into living rooms everywhere; the sudden proliferation of couture and interior decor; the ascendancy of touts and promoters; the first tendrils of professionalization in places where it never belonged; the avant-garde attempting, with varying rates of success, to make itself mass-market; the growing belief that bohemia looked less like *Pull My Daisy* and more like *Sweet Smell of Success.*

I felt adrift. So many of my friends were unavailable, for a whole catalog of reasons of their own. I went to most things by myself now. The last club I attended regularly was the Roxy, a roller disco in the West Twenties that one night a week covered the rink and welcomed the Manhattan hip-hop–postpunk interface. It was the first club I'd ever seen with coin lockers, a major advance for civilization; you no longer needed to worry about your coat getting swiped. And the place was big and airy—you could have fit three Mudd Clubs inside. Afrika Bambaataa was on the decks, and he was maybe high all the time? Certainly not the most attentive or consistent of DJs; given to abrupt transitions, sometimes right as a number was peaking. One night he played "UFO" by ESG, one of my favorites, at least a dozen times in succession. It was a fitting last club for me,

the culmination of all my local musical paths over the years finally merging into one. After that I pretty much stopped paying attention.

I had a connection at the renascent *Vanity Fair*, and was given the
opportunity to profile whomever I chose. I suggested Neil Young,
but they said, That old hippie? Then I suggested Jacques Rivette
and they said yes. I arranged to see all his movies again, through the
kind offices of Jackie Raynal, and I read all his press and even managed to obtain his home number. I knew he would be starting to
shoot a picture very soon. I had prepared for the assignment the way
I would have for a piece in the *Review*, hoovering up every available
bit of information, but I was too naive or feral or simply stupid to
think of, say, writing a letter to his production company to say I was
coming. In my world you yelled up at the window and they threw
down the keys wrapped in a sock.

So I went to Paris and spent two weeks dialing his number, from
nine a.m. to nine p.m. Years later Jim told Rivette what had happened, and he laughed. "They didn't know I only answer the phone
after midnight." I stayed with two couples, friends of a friend, up in
the northeast corner by the canal. They were skillful and accomplished thieves, who had extra-deep pockets sewn into their clothes.
They'd come back from the store and pull choice cuts of meat and
bottles of champagne from unusual regions of their leather coats.
Sometimes they'd haul out nonculinary items as well. Did I think

this (large, remarkably engraved) piece of scrimshaw was real? I asked what they did to pay the rent, and one of them said "construction"; I saw no evidence of construction. They taught me how to play a viciously aggressive game of poker in French, took me around to ancient billiard halls and *estaminets* that wouldn't be there the next time I made it to Paris, introduced me to a venerable sex worker who had been photographed by Brassaï. They were former high school Enragés from 1972 who now practiced the anarchist doctrine of "individual reprisal"—all capital was stolen goods, so theft from high-end shops was just a take-back (they did pay for their vegetables at the market). They gave me reading lists too; later three of the four would each start their own radical press. Those two weeks were yet another education for me, one that launched three dozen lines of inquiry I would later pursue.

My love life was disastrous, as usual. Eva's former roommate arrived one day, calling from the airport, with the clear intention of moving in with me. I panicked. I pretended I was sick and sent her away. I was relieved, but I was suffused with shame for a long time, with the result that when the next person who was clearly wrong for me knocked on my door, I opened it. She was a friend; I enjoyed her company; together we had a line in comic repartee. And she came from another world. With her I went to gallery dinners, and fancy restaurants on others' dimes, and dinners in lofts at tables that sat sixteen. But our hearts were in very different places, and I knew it from the start. I passively allowed our relationship to proceed out of emotional paralysis and the fear of being alone. Very soon the contradictions began to assert themselves. I started drinking too much, and red wine made me angry. I had words with others, raised my voice, stormed out. Afterward I'd go alone to random clubs where they didn't charge admission and sit in the corner getting drunker while listening to seven bad punk bands end to end. After she moved in with me I came home from work one day to discover that she had gone through my closet and pulled everything that displeased her, everything worn or torn or weird or in her view outmoded. My punk-era gear, the jackets I'd inherited from my father, things with deep associations that were going to stay in my closet even if I never wore them again: all of them were in the trash or at Goodwill. Two-thirds of my clothes were gone. The term for her action is "soul murder." I was so depressed I didn't even have the strength to throw her out. In fact I later married her.

I do seem to have attracted a certain kind of person who wanted to edit me, who perhaps figured that I came with a number of negotiable qualities—well mannered, well spoken, highly if unconventionally educated, regular features, average body type—that might or might not compensate for my liabilities. I was driven, but not by remunerative ambitions. I was cosmopolitan, but relentlessly downmarket. I loved hanging out, but I hated sitting around. I could drink brandy and smoke cigars with the men, but I had nothing to say to them. I preferred the grimiest parts of cities to places with nice houses and greenery. I hated everybody's family. I hated holidays, seasonal festivities, country weekends, group vacations, family traditions, school reunions, benefit committees, professional friendships, assigned seating, small-town society, big-city society, competitive consumership, social obligations, rituals of any sort, conformity on any scale, any unelected relationship, any imbalance of power. I was not clubbable, not a joiner, not a regular or a habitué, not one of the gang, not going to be your best buddy anytime soon. I was friendly but distant, wishing I were anywhere but wherever I was.

I was a writer, of course, and a writer's life is never very interesting, because so much of it takes place inside the writer's head. As I look back over the more recent decades I find that some of my strongest, most visceral memories are of projects. If I've actually written the book the experience is contained and distilled in that book, but I feel a strange nostalgia for all those deep investigations, some of them lasting years, that never amounted to anything much: tramps and hobos, New Orleans jazz, the end of the silent era, the newspaper culture of the past, the anarchist tradition, the world of exiles. I remember those as if they were places where I once lived. I walked around in them and felt at home. That wasn't writing, of course, but the immersion that would have preceded it. Writing itself, when it worked, was like being a spirit medium. It wasn't a process you could share with anyone. You could only share its result, which Walter Benjamin said was the death mask of its inspiration.

I spent middle age behind a wall. I was in deep denial of more than just my gender. I was going through the motions of life as if I were operating it by remote control. Even my old friendships seemed to flag in those years; I couldn't reach out to anyone about anything. I was usually coupled—I divorced and remarried—but unhappy, feeling isolated in my household and isolated outside it. I wasn't even unfaithful, except once as a deliberate terminal action. I felt as alone as I had at the beginning of puberty. I had a poisonous tendency to turn my spouses into my mother, the one of my adolescence, and they obliged. I became a father myself, and tried hard at it because I loved my son, although I suspect I acted much as my own father had—a combination of benign neglect and well-meaning wrong-footedness—and I felt utterly miscast in the role. My mistrust of families was total; I had never known a good one. Because I had moved upstate my distance from my old friends was now geographic as well as emotional. My resentment of arbitrary relationships— with neighbors, colleagues, other parents—was at its height, be- cause I was starting to believe that I no longer had anything in common with anyone else. My discontent with my gender was as deep as it ever had been, and as ever I couldn't name it to myself, especially since I was now so old I had to set all my fantasies in the past.

I was rescued from my near-suicidal track by an invitation to the newly constituted one-hundred-member chat group, which happily coincided with my finally getting my own laptop after sharing a

desktop with my spouse for ten years. All of a sudden I had ninety-nine potential friends, not nearby but available, most of them somewhat younger than me, many of them smart and funny. There were little clusters of previous acquaintanceship in the group, but most of us didn't know the others, and for at least five years the group percolated as we all tried to figure one another out. I met Mimi early on, and then I really felt like I was busting out of jail. I became social in a way I hadn't been for over two decades; at one point I'd met three-quarters of the group in person (the membership has fluctuated). After about six months of courtship Mimi and I bought a house near where I had been living—I couldn't move far from my son—and she got a job at Bard, and soon was introducing me to colleagues I'd never met, who promptly became my friends. This reentry into the world was my first rebirth. Thirteen years would pass before my second.

By September, coming out had become an addiction. By then it had become less about letting people know and more about experiencing myself telling them, which reminded me that it was real. I wasn't always sure that I hadn't lapsed into a coma and devised this remarkable dream existence for myself out of nothing. It was high time I cemented it by telling the whole world, or at least the portion of it that followed me on Instagram, my sole social medium. I posted a goofy selfie taken at my desk and told the story as briefly and plainly as I could. And very quickly I got all kinds of response, cartloads of likes, scads of new followers, a wave of "hidden requests" from guys named Butch whose messages consisted entirely of "Hey." Within twenty-four hours I had four invitations to tell my tale for publication. I went with *Vanity Fair* because I liked and trusted David Friend, my editor, and also because I thought I might get a glam photo shoot out of it.

Somehow, though, in my delirium I had overlooked something critical. For reasons I'm at a loss to supply, I staged my coming-out on Mimi's birthday. I remain baffled by this. Hurting her was the very last thing I wanted, but I did. I can only surmise that it was my unconscious avenging my own pain, although somewhat disproportionately. We had gone through two rounds of couples therapy. The first I had botched by spending most of the sessions in tears, unable to focus on the exercises the therapist assigned us, and the second wasn't much better; Mimi remained cogent throughout. We conducted the sessions over Zoom, sitting side by side on the banquette in the kitchen. Seeing both of us in the frame made me wince; Mimi was a real woman while I was a pretend woman. I knew full well, deep inside, that the terms of our relationship and the differing styles of our personalities were not conducive to continuing a romantic relationship under the changed conditions. But I couldn't come to terms with that fact because I was overcome with a feeling of abandonment, my most reliable trigger. I was so vulnerable to that sensation that I had always, barring only Eva, done the leaving myself.

Maybe I simply wasn't meant to be with anyone. That was the pattern of my life, after all. I knew how to be alone, had studied the matter deeply, knew all the shadings of aloneness, had even spent considerable time alone within each of my relationships, but I was afraid to be alone. And I had hurt Mimi, whom I loved in the most clearheaded way. After thirteen years the initial flame of romance may have come to burn low, but I loved her in great detail: everything she said and did, pretty much, and the way she looked and the way she moved. And those feelings were unlikely to change. Mimi's forthrightness was consistent and pure; deception was not in her toolbox. For me her blunt honesty became an example and a rule, and gave me a new optic for judging my own sentences. Mimi never tailored her speech or behavior to her auditors. She spoke the same way to the cashier and the college president, the beggar and the celebrity, refusing to talk up or down even when it might have benefited her to do so—I'm guessing she may have flunked some job interviews for failing to employ the expected speech codes. She was ABD in linguistics, so it's not as if she were unaware of how she sounded. She knew how to use words better than almost anyone I've known; she came to writing later in life, but arrived fully formed.

She was an old-school democrat and a Jewish Midwestern Boston Yankee who hated waste, was suspicious of anything she deemed "fancy"—you don't need that expensive slogan T-shirt; she'll buy a cheap plain one at Walmart and draw it for you—and constantly had one project or another going, in every domain (home repair, linocuts, blackcap jelly, baby quilts, stained glass, short stories, cherry pies, tiny paintings), all of which she brought to brilliant completion, exactly according to plan. And she was eternally cute, sexily insouciant, somehow still partly teenaged decades after the fact. Do you wonder why I hated losing her? But she too knew that we couldn't not be friends. We ran way too deep to just drift apart.

When the semester started, I began presenting full-time. Naturally, none of my students gave a rat's ass. I generally found it easy in everyday life—with COVID-mask subterfuge when applicable—except at the dog park. People and dogs recurred there, but not with enough consistency for the humans, at least, to form bonds. People were neither friendly nor unfriendly, but I imagined they were puzzled. I wished that someone would have asked me what the deal was, but all conversation was dog-related, and I wasn't about to launch into talking about myself unprompted. I was consumed by the need to explain myself to everyone. My transition was rarely the subject of comment among my friends and acquaintances. Now and then someone would tell me I looked good, but that was the extent of it. My very closest people would naturally hear me tell all because with them I could talk unprompted, but the others maybe were too creeped out or frightened or bored to ever ask me how things were going. How's life now that you're sixteen feet tall? Is the weather different? How do you sleep?

But really it's that many cis people (I first wrote "civilians") are baffled by transgender matters, no matter how nice they may be to transgender people. For those who haven't experienced it, gender dysphoria is a hard thing to conceptualize. It may be difficult for them to understand that sex and gender are not identical propositions, and it is certainly hard for them to understand the urgency and totality of the need. Not understanding the why and the how will make people a bit frightened. Delicacy and the wish not to hurt may prevent them from articulating the sort of questions they actually want to ask: How did we not know that about you? Will you be dating men now? How do you feel about your dick? If not: Wasn't it taboo only yesterday? Doesn't it run contrary to nature? Isn't it something you'd see in sideshows? Isn't identity just a construct after all? In any case, most of the people in my life preferred to act as if nothing had happened. If we normally talked about movies or music or local gossip or animals, we'd carry on talking about movies or music or local gossip or animals. That was fine as far as it went, but after a while it made me feel a bit sexless and unappreciated. I was, after all, on a metaphysical journey that beggared anything they were likely to have experienced.

The peculiarities of age mean that I can easily feel twenty-seven down to my toes, and at the same time recognize that a great gulf separates me from my youth. The world is utterly changed and no circumstance can ever be as it was before. I didn't think I'd ever end up where I am, in more ways than one. I've always been intensely superstitious about gazing into the future, have always avoided sooth-sayers, cards, tea leaves, for all that they were most likely bogus—I never wanted to know. My visions of my future were glancing and unintentional and came in only three flavors. There was some woo-zily imagined glory with none of the background sketched in, and variegated nightmares of failure and destruction, and what I thought was actually realistic: that I might have some coterie success but would spend my life just scraping by, living in leaky tenements and working part-time in bookstores, still as feckless and untethered as ever. Often I'd stop and stare in wonder at the idea that I actually had become a functioning adult, up-to-date on bills, halfway through a thirty-year mortgage, putting a child through college, getting my furnace inspected, renewing my homeowner's insurance, planning a dinner three days in advance, all those things you eventually have to do, assuming you can, that sound like death to the young mind. That seemed hard to accept, considering that my mind was still the same exact chaos it had been at seventeen.

The world had changed, but I didn't feel as though I had changed with it. My marriages were succeeding monarchies, the profile of each determining the cast of their time. This one was the 1980s: we ate at restaurants where you were served seven squid-ink ravioli on a plate the size of a bicycle wheel, wore clothes with shoulders that extended three inches past that corner of the body, were always onto the new thing six months before the general public, went in on group summer-house rentals in eastern Long Island, went out for brunch and tried fad cocktails and knew the names of liquor-company publicists. That one was the 1990s: we joined a food co-op and experimented with previously unknown leafy greens, drove a Subaru wagon with snarky bumper stickers, spent months touring upstate properties with real estate agents, gave each other Mexican *calaveras* purchased at the hipster novelty store, socialized over potluck suppers around fire rings, talking about stuff we'd read in advice columns. I underwent all these things passively; they were weather. But at the same time they seemed alien, and my participation ceremonial, as if I were visiting a foreign country and for diplomatic reasons had to undergo all the observances, however inexplicable.

I missed my old friends and jumped at any chance to see them; a party that would bring us all together happened twice a year, tops. But our common timeline had fractured; each of us was pursuing an individual plot wildly different from all the others, and each of us now possessed spheres of life the others couldn't know. Darryl was in the UK, before that Berlin, sometimes Paris or New York; he had met James, who turned out to be just who he was looking for. Alexis was married and had two kids, had bought the adjacent apartment and merged the two, had sold her bathroom door and her refrigerator door, both painted by Jean-Michel. Felice was struggling to raise her son, Seth, alone, while starting her band, Faith NYC. Jim and Sara were making movies and mingling with the jet set. Suzanne, ever the shoe fetishist, was selling them at Charles Jourdan and acting in the rough-and-ready downtown queer theater of those days. Cynthia had put the Bush Tetras on pause while she taught school and raised her son, Austin. In the forest in the Central African Republic, Louis was living with the Bayaka pygmies and recording their music.

Not long after my last visit to San Francisco, in 1982, Eva started writing to me about odd physical sensations she was having. She felt something malign emanating from television, and began having to avoid apartments and bars where the sets were left on. Then she started experiencing the same queasy sensations from the neighbors' TV, right through the wall, and after a while those persisted even when the set was turned off. She described the sensations as "allergies." Soon the allergies expanded to include all recently manufactured items. I was always sending her packages, and she requested that I leave anything new, such as books, out on the fire escape for a few days before mailing. The list kept expanding;

everything made her sick. Eventually she was diagnosed with multiple sclerosis.

Her decline was swift. On her last visit east, in 1990, I had to pay for a car service to bring her to the city from her mother's house on the Jersey shore, and then I carried her up to my apartment. At some point she lost the ability to write, so we talked by phone, but then she lost the ability to speak. If the phone rang and I heard silence on the other end, I'd improvise a dialogue in a vacuum. In 1998 I toured my book *The Factory of Facts*, with fewer people at each successive stop, until I hit the end, a bookstore on the Berkeley-Oakland line, attended by five, one of whom I had asked to come. I was shocked by the changes in San Francisco; money had clamped down. I went to visit Eva at her apartment in the Inner Sunset. She had blue hair. And she smiled, weakly, mostly with her eyes. Everything else about her was inert, as if deflated. I was happy to have seen her, but it was devastating to look upon her ruin. She died a couple of months later, when she lost the ability to breathe. I've never stopped memorializing her. I even typed up our complete correspondence and had two copies bound at OfficeMax. (Neither copy, at this writing, can be found.) She remains a puzzle that will not allow itself to be solved.

My father was diagnosed with Parkinson's disease seemingly the day after he retired in 1987. For quite a few years all that meant was that he'd keep his shaky right hand in his pocket. By the late nine-

ties, though, things had gone dramatically south. By then I was visiting my parents weekly and taking them shopping. One day I was
sitting with my father in the car while my mother was getting a prescription filled. He began telling me about a childhood memory,
something evoked in him by the snowy landscape outside—when
his speech broke up as if the needle had skipped across the record.
He never made sense again after that. My mother enrolled him in
dementia day care, but he, the gentlest of men, was expelled for
kicking other people in the ass. Then one day he lit all the burners
on the stove and left the house. He had formerly been neurotic about
checking the burners before leaving, even if we hadn't used them in
hours. Meanwhile our dog Roscoe, found abandoned in Prospect
Park and mentally damaged by whatever he had undergone, had
snapped at the baby. We called far and wide, but could not find a
shelter to take him in. So it was that one fall morning in 1999 I took
Roscoe to the vet to be put down, then drove to New Jersey to have
my father committed.

The following year was a blur: helping raise an infant, commut-
ing upstate to teach undergraduates (certain that I would sooner or
later be fired for incompetence), trying to keep up with the writing
that remained my principal source of income, visiting endless cubi-
cles in state geriatric service agencies, meeting with social workers
and lawyers, touring assisted-living facilities with my mother, who
eventually decided on the same nursing home as my father, in that

little patch of woods where I'd smoked pot during lunch hour in high school. My father, who by then had retreated into an unbreakable silence, remained in a different room. My mother called frequently to complain about everything. My son Raphael's birthday was September 11, and it was arranged that the day after he turned two I would drive him down to visit my parents. When that day arrived the world had changed, however, and I had to call my mother to tell her the visit had to be postponed. The trouble was that I couldn't tell her why, since bad news—news in general—was concealed from the inmates of the home. But I couldn't drive down there, not with a small child, not when everybody was waiting for the other shoe to drop. As I haltingly tried to construct an excuse, my mother swore and cursed at me, and then hung up. A few days later an attendant at the home called to tell me she had died, of congestive heart failure. It seemed fitting that our contact would end with her cursing me. My father followed two and a half months later, having refused food and drink for a week, a mode of death known as "Alzheimer's suicide." Since his eyes never focused, I never had any idea what was in his head in his years of silence, whether he took anything in as I wheeled him to watch my mother's coffin being lowered into the grave. The timing made me think he had taken in more than I suspected, and I felt stricken that I had treated him as if he were merely a shell with an absent host.

My body delivered one sob for each of my parents, immediately

after each phone announcement, a sob that began somewhere around my intestines and burst upward and out of my throat as if controlled by some other agency, as my back slowly slid down the wall. And that was it. I was sad and I was relieved. Dealings with my mother had been painful until the very end. We hated each other so intensely it was almost like love. Although she stopped hitting me when I turned eighteen, her acrimony actually seemed to increase with the years, even when I was performing the midlife petit-bourgeois heterosexual ideal. She was utterly unimpressed by my work and indifferent to how it was received. She could not abide something that had come out of her womb that was not another her, and she laid blame on me for everything that was wrong with her life. My father cared for me and understood me more than she did, but the problem there was that I didn't know who he was. I knew his moods, his party acts, his sentimentality, his smatterings of culture, his repertoire of jokes, but I also suspected there was an iceberg below those waters, even though I couldn't say why. Maybe because I never met his dead friends, or because he sometimes seemed to project worldliness not borne out by his biography. Maybe it was partly because I knew so little about his family, only two others of which I ever met, one of whom died when I was four.

The other, my Tante Armande, ten years older than my father, was a large, sweet, shy woman who never said much in her delicate little piping voice as she brought in the steaming *tête de veau*, using the corners of her apron as pot holders. Joseph Peerboom, her Dutch topiary-gardener husband, who as well as being my uncle was economically also my godfather, did all the talking, as he mixed his scotch with apricot schnapps. After his death and maybe a year before her own, Armande burned all the family papers. Even my father didn't know why, or for that matter what exactly they contained. Was she simply crazy? Or was she covering something up? I will never know, and I feel as I did when I was fourteen and gullible, reading about Atlantis: an entire world disappeared with no trace. Her action preceded by a year my mother's destruction of my childhood, and followed by a year or two the destruction of my clothes by my first wife.

You get no points for connecting all this to my mania for preservation and archiving. There was also the loss of the contents, destroyed in transit, of some of the famous nine crates of belongings that accompanied my parents and me when we first ventured to the New World. Also for that matter the loss of an entire old world across the ocean, which my mother could only helplessly observe in snippets from afar as it collapsed and changed into something else, more like America and less like a village, losing the old habits and expressions and beliefs of a mode of life just one generation removed from the soil. Those losses I heard about ceaselessly, within a dinner-table discourse that always inexorably wound in the direction of doom, from above and from below. When we lived under a flight path to Newark airport in the early 1960s, I was sure that every plane I heard overhead was about to drop bombs on us. (Even now, when the news is bad, my mind is immediately filled with images of panicked escape, just like in 1940.) And the world was presided over by the god of doom, who might have been a creator but seemed to enjoy sending people to hell above all else.

When I first started trying to move out from under this shadow, around age ten, I was powered by books and music and my fourth-grade teacher, Mrs. Gibbs, the first person to tell me I had writing talent, who once a week took us down to Holy Name Hall, where she instructed us in square dancing—and then threw caution to the wind, plugged in the jukebox, and taught us to frug to "My Boy-friend's Back" by the Angels. Dancing to pop music gave me proof that there was a better world somewhere. I picked up this world in bits and pieces because I was a child, but it wasn't hard to find in the mid-1960s. Glamour would suddenly walk by, as if just landed from a spaceship. Danger, a close associate of Glamour, lurked around the corner inspecting its fingernails. I saw it in magazines and heard it on the radio, which in those days meant a great collective ambient radio, at least in the cities. I slowly assembled the beginnings of a self and a world from flotsam and jetsam that appealed to me. My con-ceit was that I was self-created. In my mind I was a feral child, like the wild boy of Aveyron, unadapted to the life of my own species, who one day finds the wreckage of an airliner in the forest and pieces together knowledge of the human world from its surviving contents. I wasn't really sure what school was for, besides day care. I was vitally interested in education, but that didn't seem to be going on there.

I maintained this conceit forever with myself, even though I had many great teachers of all sorts throughout my youth, in and out of school. (I had some real stinkers too.) In doing so I was perhaps demonstrating my thorough absorption of the American ideal; I was rehearsing my eventual success story. The thing nobody could really help me with, though, was how to construct a self I could send out into the world, amid colliding sets of garbled and incomplete instructions from different corners of my life. Everything seemed arbitrary. I could mimic this or that specific behavior, but couldn't sufficiently understand the underlying logic to knit the behaviors into a convincing personality. With the help of my friends I did eventually manage to have some kind of life, rather than living in a container behind the supermarket and numerologically decoding the phone book. I managed to impersonate someone answering to my biographical specifics and adhering to the behavioral codes of the class I had willy-nilly joined, as if I were a George Saunders character performing in a living-history exhibit. Meanwhile I espoused an ethic of rigorous honesty in my life and work, supposedly permitting no bullshit in my writing or behavior, even as I was aware of being less than candid about myself. I didn't yet know that gender dysphoria would be the Rosetta stone that finally tied the whole mess together.

$\bigcirc$

So now here I am, just shy of eighteen months of hormone replacement therapy at this writing. I am legally Lucy, certified female, out to every single person in my life, however remote. I haven't presented as male for any reason for well over a year. I've traveled quite a lot—fifteen airports in eight months—on my deadname and dudface passport without a hitch. I was finally booted off the pink cloud once and for all just over six months ago. I've spent those six months mostly working, to make up for lost time. In other words, I'm totally normal, the same person as ever, while also quite different. (Transitioning really makes you appreciate the beauty of the dialectic.) I miss the wild highs of that first year, but they were not meant to be sustained. As with a house settling into its foundation, those early changes have gradually been absorbed and adapted by my personality. I'm socially at ease as never before, but I'm still a loner who will at some point stray from the party to go sit by myself, and I will spend big chunks of time apart from others, because that's how I do my work. I still buy too many clothes, but my purchases are more focused, now that I know better who I am. I'm on full alert in public places—I lived through the 1970s in New York City, so it's second

nature—but nonetheless I just brazen my way through public interactions of any sort; I've never, for instance, tried to alter the sound of
my baritone voice. I've been stared at plenty, but have faced zero
aggression, because I don't represent a threat: I'm old, white, and
reasonably privileged. My second puberty expired without real ca-
sualties. (One disastrous date and my illusions fried like a moth on
a lamp.)

I can honestly say that I'm happy, in a way I've never been before. I am finally inhabiting myself, the shadow me once hidden
under the floorboards. I feel entirely comfortable, as if I had always
been this way in waking life. I actually do feel free of the neuroses
that plagued me forever. I can and will of course be sad, for many
reasons, but depression is at least at bay for now. I'm old, and that's
unfortunate, although I'm exceedingly lucky: on some days in certain kinds of light I don't look my age. I naturally wish I could have
transitioned in my teens, or my twenties, or any age earlier than
mine, but there are compensations: being left in peace, remaining
immune to all affinity-group competition, being able to nestle my
changes into a life that was already structured, having outlived all
the censorious elders. I genuinely like who I am—I'm turning out
better than I'd imagined, or feared. Naturally I can't see myself.
Back in pink-cloud days, I often suspected the mirror of being in-
fested with pixie dust—and untreated selfies exist to bear out my
suspicions. But my mirror had to lie to me to shield me from the

blistering truth, which might have halted me in my tracks. Nowadays photography and the mirror may be a little more in accord, perhaps having signed a secret treaty. That even extends sometimes to pictures taken by other people.

It has been a year and nine months since my egg cracked, and still the authenticity debate proceeds continuously in a corner of my mind, like a succession case stuck in an infinite loop in probate court. I'm deeply fatigued by the argument, which never changes except in tone. Some days it's hard to distinguish among principled inquiry, existential house inspection, nervous-Nelly doublechecking, and internalized transphobia. Anyway my legal team presents the same defense argument again and again, conclusively every time: this was always who I was, and here are 164 exhibits as proof. I am of course well aware that I owe no entity, imaginary or otherwise, any kind of explanation, let alone evidence, but while that might fly with my intellect, just try convincing my emotions. My nerves are still keyed up, although I no longer notice the crackle.

I know that my emotions have changed, have risen closer to the surface in many ways. I'll always be fated to disappoint the acquaintance who fervently hoped that transition would make me, and by extension my writing, "more emotional." By that she meant that I should perform emotion with large gestures on a big gold set, but that isn't me. I'm a minimalist by nature when it comes to conveying feelings; I assume that to be an inherited, perhaps ethnic trait rather

than anything gender-connected. I'm certainly more conscious of others, at all times, and I find it far easier to bring up emotional matters with them (when I do, it sometimes feels like a breach of decorum, because it runs so much against established grain). Often, in varied circumstances, I experience a kind of serenity, a general rightness with the world, an acceptance of my being and my eventual fate now that I finally have achieved true selfhood. I don't hate myself anymore, am no longer apologetic for my very existence. I walk with pride. I feel exceptionally fortunate, grateful to whatever force cracked my egg before it was too late. I was saved from drowning.

It's been fascinating watching my maleness dry up. Because they were just assumed protective behaviors, most of my masculine traits and attributes—ways of inhabiting my body, attitudes toward others—vanished like cockroaches when you turn on the light. There remained my inner narrative profile, that unnoticed but constant wax dummy, which was more tenacious because absorbed at a deeper level; it has been dissolving slowly over a year and a half. I was as delighted to stop being a man as I was to become a woman. I found that I saw and heard men differently now. It wasn't that I'd ever consciously thought of myself as a man among men, or felt solidarity with males in any targeting of their gender, or had any reaction when op-ed writers bemoaned some example of the unmanning of society. In my male days, walking into a room filled with guys would have been the opposite of reassuring. Walking into a guy-filled room now is a neutral experience, because all the territorial menace is gone (and the predatory menace is absent because I'm old). Nowadays, observing men and their words and actions is like reading a familiar text in another language—perhaps the original. Everything is immediately subject to semiotic cryptanalysis; the nominal content is far less significant than its framing. The results are by turns boring, hilarious, and alarming, as you'd expect. Objectification is fun, as long as no one gets hurt.

Symmetrically, I now feel women's concerns as my own, in a way that wasn't previously available to me. I was obviously always on the side of women, but only now, when faced with a lineup of writers or artists, say, do I seek out the women first without even thinking about it. I feel that I have joined the team as an associate member, and I am youthfully eager to support the side. Women's pain means something different to me now. Random small interactions with women—on the checkout line at the supermarket, in the waiting room at the doctor's—have taken on an entirely different cast. One thing I'm certain helped lead me to this moment was when *Kill All Your Darlings*, my first collection of essays, was reviewed in *The Nation* by Frances Richard, who pointed out that all the subjects were men. I was abashed. I hadn't realized. That led me to examining the place of female writers and artists in my life. So many were of critical importance to me, and yet my writing about writers and artists centered on the males, because I had unconsciously subscribed to the dick-matching ethos that still prevailed. Men's work was serious, a life-or-death struggle to reach the top. Women's work, in the world I entered in my youth, was always asterisked, italicized, special-categoried, exceptions made for, not entered in the main competition. Even allowing for the ridiculous dichotomy, it made a lot more sense for me to gravitate toward the asterisked, simply by temperament. Did I think I was enrolled in the main event? By failing to write novels I had already chosen to be a nonstarter. I slowly came to realize how unmale my creative instincts really were.

But are they female? I don't know, because I don't actually know any better than you what is female and what is male when it comes to the subjective. (I suppose, really, that there are two kinds of humans—aggressors and resisters, you might say, and that those categories very loosely overlap with the gender division as it has been understood.) There is gender playacting, deliberate or unconscious, and the rest is a broad field of ambiguity. There is an awful lot of playacting going on, to be sure, which disguises the pervasiveness of ambiguity. But playacting of some sort is a feature of any human enterprise, even and perhaps especially the ones that involve no clothes. Obviously playacting looms large in my transition, as it would in any life-changing scenario, something I learned when I was very young. (Frankly, becoming Lucy is like gliding on satin sheets compared to what it was like becoming American Luc.) When I say that I have transitioned from male to female, one of the things I mean is that I have built myself a new persona, appropriate to my age and walk of life, with a certain distinctive appearance. I didn't exactly plan this look—it just happened, but it is strong, and it instructs me on the character I am to play. I have an expectation of myself based on how I appear. My appearance is there for me to grow into.

No, my dysphoria was never centered on or even especially concerned with genitalia. (Although it is extremely exciting to have tits.) No, I didn't play with dolls as a child (I had my stuffed animals instead), and never insisted on certain colors (I'm partially colorblind). I never hated my body so much I wanted to kill it (except I did, and I can show you the scars).* I didn't have sisters or neighbor girls to play with me and dress me up, or anyone at all in my life who might have encouraged my feminine tendencies, my mother notwithstanding. I don't fit the classic transsexual profile, for whatever that's worth. To give an account of what makes me female would be like trying to define femininity without reference to reproduction. Once past the playacting, what is there? It's a way of being in a

---

*In the summer of 1977, while I was living with Jim and George on 101st Street, I got into a strange state. I had the refrain to that Sex Pistols song on repeat in my head: "No future." I felt that I had none, that my life was over, that I had failed to qualify as a human being. In a paroxysm of rage I began smashing the panels on the French door to my room with my fist. Almost immediately my wrist caught a shard of glass on the way back out, and was spurting jets of blood. My roommates came running and hustled me to the emergency room. All the while I kept repeating to myself that I hadn't intended to cut my wrist. I was terrified they'd throw me in the loony bin. It was just an accident and there was nothing at all wrong with me. I may have been coherent enough to say that to the attendants, who saw no reason to doubt me.

room, of moving through a space, of seeing the world, of organizing place and time, of the urge to give, of connectedness to others, of moral responsibility, of representing truth—of everything on earth, that is, but with a specific vibration, a particular energy that can only be defined by a pileup of examples (see the works of Colette, for example). There are female characteristics that I already felt within myself all my life, and there are others that I am absorbing as I change. Transitioning is not an event but a process, and it will occupy the rest of my life as I go on changing.

I am a transgender woman, which legally and ethically should be recognized as identical to the cisgender kind, but in practice means that I am and will remain something of a woman-in-training, at least in the eyes of the world and in the cobwebbed recesses of my own outlook, formed in ignorance long ago. At the same time, though, I am a fully fledged and accredited transgender woman, complete unto myself and no fucks given. Whenever I contemplate a gender-related course of action, I ask myself whether I'm basing it on my own happiness or on the judgment of others. (Should I have my vocal cords shaved? It would make daily life much easier. But that would be bowing to external pressures. On the other hand, wouldn't it be great to translate my voice into a higher register? I've always wanted to sound like Lauren Bacall. But what if it's expensive or painful or even dangerous? And so on.) Gender is of course a spectrum, but my needle is solidly in the F realm. My emotions, formed long ago, remain binary. And my experience passing as male was sufficiently painful that I don't need any souvenirs hanging around as part of my presentation—although some may cling on, above or below my eyesight. I'm not really very concerned with what you might call authenticity, at least these days. I'm more preoccupied with taste, because taste has always been the way I demonstrate that I'm as valid as anyone else.

I still haven't made many forays into trans world. I know a dozen or so trans women, only two or three of them in non-superficial ways—but they have been vital to my health and happiness. I'm old, of course, live in the hinterlands, don't possess anything like the social energy of people a third my age, which is most trans women. I obviously didn't grow up hearing the conversation on gender that marked their youth. I'm allergic to theory and even more to the kind of shibboleth rhetoric (and its principal by-product, a defensive posture) that pervades much—though by no means all—of trans writing. In the spirit of my friend Darryl, who years ago declared that he was not a gay writer but a writer who is gay, I am a writer who is trans. There is nothing of the politician about me. I don't wish to be a spokesperson, although I accept that by writing this book I will have become just that. I have faithfully recorded as many of my doubts and contradictions and mistakes and foibles and high-handed attitudes as I could remember, just to keep things in perspective. I certainly hope that my story will be read by people who need to see that gender dysphoria, expressed in childhood or adolescence, is not a passing fancy that will evaporate when the social climate changes. Not only am I lucky to have had my egg crack at something close to the last minute, I'm also lucky to have survived my own repression. I suspect that many in my position have not.

I've spent much of my life being the exception—the only child, the only immigrant, the only teenager on the 7:15 express, the only working-class kid, the only pedestrian, the only virgin, the only boy. Now, in my long-standing immediate social world, I am the only trans person. But I have also become part of something else. My story is not a typical trans story—but what is a typical trans story? All of us became aware at some point that our assigned gender did not match our inner gender, and sooner or later we found the ability to take action. There are very likely many more of us, who for now cannot or will not take action, than anyone imagines. It is clear from the historical record and from various non-Western cultures that there have always been people like us, although very few expressed their transness because of the exceptionally strong taboo. That taboo was a detail in the male campaign to hold and exercise power; there was to be no blurring of the line, or heaven forbid, deserters. It has loosened in some parts of the world because society has changed, because horizontal and vertical mobility have altered the kinship structures that dominated society for millennia and consigned people to rigid roles. But there is strong hostile reaction in many nations, now being fanned by every kind of malignant slander. We are in danger, particularly Black trans women and the indigent and homeless—there are many of these, because we often have a hard time finding work that isn't sex work, which has its own dangers.

I am the person I feared most of my life. I have, as they say, gone there. I spent most of my life ambitious but afraid: wanting notice but not too much, wanting my works to be known, but not me (even though the one theme that unified my work was, in fact, me). Repression was like a home invader who compelled me under threat to draw the curtains, answer the phone and act pleasant, cancel the dinner party, tell the people at the door to go away. And now suddenly I have all this attention. As a result of my *Vanity Fair* piece, I've been interviewed dozens of times and photographed more often than in my entire previous career. When my last book came out in the fall of 2022, on a very locavore topic—New York City's Catskills reservoirs—I wondered whether some of the publicity and the attendance at events, both of which far surpassed my expectations, weren't due to the sideshow-attraction aspect of my presence. But, you know, I'm okay with that. I don't mind representing myself as an example of someone who has found happiness by confronting the truth. I lay in pieces for so long, but now I have, as the Mafia guys say, been made whole.

9 December 2022

ACKNOWLEDGMENTS

Thank you to: Alexis Adler, Peggy Ahwesh, Angelika Becker, Philippe Bordaz, Jem Cohen, Jen Collins, Steve Connell, Mike DeCapite, Daniella Dooling, Sara Driver, James Fenton, Suzanne Fletcher, David Friend, Signy Furiya, Josh Glenn, Nan Goldin, Andrea Grunblatt, Malu Halasa, Joy Harris, Veda Hille, June Hony, Jim Jarmusch, Jennifer Jazz, Chelsey Johnson, Mandy Keifitz, Barbara Klar, Bud Kliment, Phil Kline, Shakti LaGow, Alix Lambert, Ann Lauterbach, Les LeVeque, Mimi Lipson, Alex Brook Lynn, Mike McGonigal, Leor Miller, Jamie Nares, Annie Nocenti, Gary Panter, Magdalen Pierrakos, Raphael Pierson-Sante, Darryl Pinckney, Pat Place, Catherine Puglisi, Kelly Reichardt, Frances Richard, Felice Rosser, Dmitry Samarov, Keith Sanborn, Noah Shapiro, Lisa Shea, Jordon Soper, Janet Stein, Megumi Tamaki-Seiffert, Marina van Zuylen, Cynthia Werthamer, George Winslow, Cynthia Womersley, and the crew at Love Hair in Kingston, New York.